LIVINGSTONE
THE PATHFINDER

ILLUSTRATED
BY

KURT WIESE

LIVINGSTONE
THE
PATHFINDER

1344

Basil Mathews

New edition

FRIENDSHIP PRESS
NEW YORK

LIBRARY OF CONGRESS CATALOG CARD NUMBER: 54-11981

NEW EDITION

First printing 1954
Second printing 1963

CONTENTS

PART I

1 : *The Boy in the Mill*

It was a wintry night in a village called Blantyre in Lanarkshire, Scotland. The roar of water filled the darkness as the river Clyde poured over the breakwater that guided a part of the swollen stream into the race that drove the machinery of the cotton mill on its left bank. The river rolled on, under the blinking windows of the houses where the working people lived, on its way toward Glasgow and the sea.

Behind one of those windows in a cozy little room, a group of children clustered round an old Highlander, their grandfather—the youngest on his knee. It was almost time for them to be in bed, but they clamored for a story.

"Tell us about Great-grandfather and the fight," they cried.

The father, Neil Livingstone, quietly reading a book, looked up as the children eagerly waited for the reply.

"Yes, tell the bairns," said their mother, Agnes, who, sitting at the fireside with candle on the table, busy

> . . . wi' her needle and her shears,
> Gar'd auld claes look amaist as weel's the new.[1]

The grandfather then began to tell for the fortieth time the tale of his father at Culloden. He told them—proudly but sadly—how his father, fighting on the side of the ancient line of kings, had swung his deadly claymore in defense of Prince Charlie and had helped to win one battle after another in the Scottish Highlands. But at last on Culloden Moor, one spring morning, the army of King George in all its force broke the ranks and spirit of the wild Highlanders and slew these children's brave great-grandfather, who preferred death to flight.

The mother would then tell them, with a smile and a shake of her head at their father, that *her* grandfather was on the other side from *his* grandfather in the fierce struggle that made Scotland wretched in the old days.

[1] Made old clothes look almost as good as new.
—Burns, "The Cotter's Saturday Night"

"Your father's people fought and harried my people," she would tell them, "but now we are all one family."

So the children would sit around her and gaze into her face, which they always believed was the most beautiful in the world. The mother would tell them about when she was a girl and the days long before that, when her grandfather was a young man.

"Your great-grandfather's name," she told them, "was Gavin Hunter, and he lived in the 'cruel, killing times' of the Covenanters. These people, because they wished to be free to worship God in the way they thought best, were driven out onto the moors and the wild hills and were killed or thrown into prison. They came together on those high moorlands, among the heather, often with snow on the ground and their hair blown in the wintry wind.

"There they read and spoke and prayed as they worshiped God. Sometimes as they did so one of them, placed on the lookout, would see dragoons on horseback galloping across the brown or purple heather, who would charge among them, killing or carrying off to prison both men and women. That will never happen again in Scotland."

Sometimes, but not very often, the father would tell the children of their two uncles who, far away in Spain, had fought in the battles of Britain and how the great Battle of Waterloo had ended the fight "two years after

5

our little Davie was born." In the village it was thought a wonderful thing that some of their own people should have been in that war. How surprised they would have been to know that this boy Davie, now working in the cotton mill, would, when he grew up, perform alone mighty feats that would make more difference to the world than all the battles in which his uncles had fought in Spain!

Then Grandfather would tell them how, on the rocky island of Ulva, out where the great Atlantic rollers boom and break on the rugged coasts of the Hebrides, he and his father and grandfathers for centuries had lived and farmed.

Among the three boys and two girls in the little home the one who was best at games and liveliest at the table was David. He was born on March 19, 1813. He had beautiful blue-gray eyes like his mother—but, unlike her, he had a very strong, healthy body. His father, Neil Livingstone, earned his living by selling tea. He was also a Sunday school teacher and was so fond of books that he was always reading in the evenings at home.

David and his brothers and sisters would play in the summertime in the fields among "the happy hills of hay." And at the different times of year they played such games as "rounders," the old form of baseball, "smugglers," "hide-and-seek," and "bools," as marbles are called in Scotland.

The father made a rule that all his children must be home from play before the door was closed, and he used to shut the door soon after sunset. One evening, after it was bolted, David, who had forgotten how late it was because he was enjoying his play so much, came home and found the door barred.

He did not cry nor hammer at the door, but, getting a piece of bread from a neighbor, he sat down to go to sleep for the night on the doorstep. When his mother began to look anxiously for David, she found him there.

The day came when David was ten years old. His father and mother were quite poor, so, at that early age, David started the journeys of his life by buttoning up his jacket, putting on his Scotch bonnet, and trudging off in the gray dawn to earn his living at the Blantyre cotton mill, working among grown men.

When David reached the mill each day at six in the morning, he went to the cotton spinning frame that he had to watch. It had great whirling reels of cotton with the thread stretching from one part of the machine to the other. Every now and then the cotton threads would break, and David's work was to seize hold of the two ends of the cotton and tie them together again. This was a simple piece of work, and it was not very exciting, going on, over and over, from six in the morning till eight at night.

David's brain itself was like a busy machine spinning

7

threads. The work of his head was as thorough as that of his fingers. He never left any loose broken ends in his thought-threads. Those that he started when he was ten stretched on as he grew up and went with him into far lands. To give his brain some thread to work upon, he took a book with him when he went to the mill and propped it up on the top of the spinning frame. As he walked from one end of the frame to the other, he would snatch a moment to read a sentence or to take a look at, say, the Latin feminine first declension, and then think it over as he worked. At his work he would say to himself *mensa* (a table), *mensæ, mensæ, mensam,* and so on; or *amo, amas, amat,* as he learned his Latin by heart. He had bought a Latin grammar book at a bookshop in Blantyre with a part of his very first week's wages. The rest of these wages he gave to his mother.

When he had finished his day's work at the mill, he went at eight o'clock at night to school to work at his books with a teacher. Even after that he would sit at home glued to the book that he was reading until his mother would jump up, sometimes as late as midnight, shut up his books, blow out his candle, and pack him off to bed.

On a holiday David and his brothers would go off on a long ramble, clambering over rocks along the river bank to search for ferns and mosses, roaming over the fields and hillsides looking for beetles and butterflies, jumping down into quarries, collecting shells, or strolling along the riverside, bathing or fishing.

One day when they had fished for quite a long time David caught a salmon. It was against the law to keep it. But he could not bring himself to throw it back into the river. So he slipped it down the leg of his brother Charlie's trousers. The villagers of Blantyre were very sympathetic with the boy as he passed with his poor, swollen leg!

David and his brothers enjoyed wandering all over the hills and valleys, streams and woods around Blantyre. The rambles helped to make him strong and able to walk a long way without getting tired.

When he was eighteen years old, his master took him away from the "piecing" work of joining the ends of broken thread and raised him to the full position of a spinner. This was very much harder work, but it was well paid. He wanted to earn more money because he had begun to weave his threads into a plan—a most difficult and fascinating plan.

2 : *The Smoke of a Thousand Villages*

Children, rambling with friends, jumping ditches and climbing trees, walking to school or work, often have many more thoughts than older people guess. They are sure to wonder what they will become when they grow up. David Livingstone was no exception. While he was spinning cotton at the mill, his busy mind was spinning wonder-threads and weaving from them a magic carpet that carried him over oceans and many strange lands. The magic travel that he loved most and enjoyed oftenest was across Europe and Persia, the Himalayas and Burma, to the country of the "Celestials," the people who thought their land was the middle kingdom of the world—the Chinese.

David had heard of a brave man with the strange name of Gutzlaff. Gutzlaff went to these people, dressed like them in Chinese clothes, gave them books to read, healed the bodies of those who were sick or wounded while he told them the story of the love of Jesus. So Gutzlaff, the doctor-missionary in China, became the hero of David, the boy in Scotland, now growing to be a young man as he worked at his spinning frame. If David had been told by some wizard, "Ask what you would most of all wish in the world, and you shall have it," he would certainly have answered quite quickly, "To go to China and work with Dr. Gutzlaff and be like him."

David Livingstone had already made a discovery. He found that Gutzlaff himself had a Hero, who had come to people as a healer and a missionary and who had led Gutzlaff out to China. David had been taught all about this great Physician. He had learned to say his name, even when a little boy, as he knelt at night by his mother's knee to say his evening prayers. Now that he had become older, David felt that the finest thing in the whole world for him was to follow in the same way and become a medical missionary. He said very often to himself, "The great God had an only Son, and he was sent to earth as a missionary. It is something

11

to be a follower in the wake of the only model missionary that ever appeared among men."

That was David's quest—that was his plan. But how could he, a spinner whose father and mother were poor, become what he wished? Money was needed, for to be a physician meant passing through years of costly training.

There was no good fairy to wave a wand and make everything come as he wished. David saw that he must be his own wizard.

When he had made up his mind to go out to the distant land to tell the story of the good Physician to those people who had never heard it, he did not at once tell everybody. He just talked about it with his father and mother and his minister. All three were glad. His mother's shining eyes would show the pain and pride that mothers feel when their sons go far away from home for the first time to face perils. It was just as brave of her to be glad to give up her son as it was of him to set his face toward so great an adventure.

Around the fire in the house at Blantyre, David talked with his father and mother about his plans for securing an education.

"I will work at the spinning all through the summer," he said, "and, if I save my wages carefully, that will give me enough money to keep myself in Glasgow in the winter, while I go to the lectures."

12

One winter's day, when the snow lay white and crisp on all the fields and hedges, Neil Livingstone, the father, and his son David left their Blantyre home and trudged along the frosty road to Glasgow. They walked together along the seven miles of road, sometimes silent, sometimes talking of how David would live as a student or of the price he must pay for the lodgings that they were now going to find.

They found very cheap lodgings after much trudging and knocking at many doors, and the father walked back home leaving his young son alone. The next day David went out and paid the £12, nearly $50, that he had saved up as fees for the lectures, and at night wrote to one of his friends saying how very lonely he felt now that his father had gone. But he added, with that indomitable spirit that was to be so characteristic of him all his life, "I must put a stout heart to a stey brae" (a stiff hill).

One day the young student David stood in Glasgow with a letter in his hand addressed to the London Missionary Society. In that letter he had written offering himself to the society for service in the foreign field. He posted it, and the answer came asking him to go to London to see the directors.

What excitement for the young student as for the first time, in 1838, he walked the streets of London and saw the wonderful sights!

13

He went on one of those days into the stately Abbey Church at Westminster, where great kings and knights and saints—the heroes of Britain—lie buried. He thought as he gazed at the many-colored windows and the marble monuments how splendid it would be to have done such deeds as theirs. He did not know, nor would anyone have imagined watching the dark-haired, sturdy-looking student as he stood there in the Abbey nave, that one day the whole vast place would be thronged in every corner with the greatest men in the land, while the world mourned for Livingstone himself, as his body was carried there to its last resting place under that very roof.

Livingstone was told by the directors of the London Missionary Society that they wished him to go through a course of training at a place called Chipping Ongar, near London, and that, if he went through that course well, they would accept him as a missionary. While there he had the following little adventure, which showed the pluck that was afterwards to carry him over thousands of miles of land and water, through marsh and forest, desert and tempest.

One foggy morning in November, before the sun had risen, he left the house at Ongar to walk to London to see one of his father's relatives. In the dense mist and the pitchy darkness he left the road and fell into the ditch, soiling his clothes. Picking himself up, he started

14

again to go on with his walk of twenty-seven miles to London. When he got there, his relative took him about the streets to see the sights.

Later in the day Livingstone, having already walked well over thirty miles, started to trudge the twenty-seven miles back to Ongar. He had not gone far on the Great North Road when he discovered a lady lying by the roadside near Edmonton. She had been thrown out of a gig as she drove along and had been stunned by the fall. With help Livingstone carried her to a house close by and, as a doctor, examined her. Then, already more than tired out, he started again on his walk.

Some miles farther on he missed his way in the darkness. He was hardly able to drag one foot after the other, and his body cried out for sleep, but he knew he dare not lie down on the roadside on that raw November night. He staggered on, found a direction post, climbed it as if it were a tree, and by the light of the stars managed to read the names on it and get back to the right road.

He reached Ongar again at midnight, twenty-one hours after he had started, having walked sixty miles. He was dead tired and as white as a sheet. After eating a bowl of bread and milk prepared by his fellow student, who helped him into bed, he slept without moving for twelve hours.

While at Ongar, Livingstone used to go for rambles with a boy called Isaac Taylor, who wrote, forty years later:

"I remember his step, the characteristic forward-tread, firm, simple, resolute, neither fast nor slow, no hurry and no dawdle, but which evidently meant getting there."

As another man who knew him at that time said, "Fire, water, stone wall would not stop Livingstone."

Suddenly, however, his path seemed to be stopped as by "fire, water, and stone wall." At the very time he was ready to start, a horrible war broke out in China, the land to which he had been commissioned to go. What should he do?

At a missionary meeting he heard, and he afterwards met, a tall man with great flowing beard, firm face, and kindly piercing eyes—Robert Moffat. Moffat had come back from the broad plains and hills of Africa—Africa, the vastest and most mysterious continent on the earth, its heart then absolutely unknown. People used to think that the interior of Africa was a desert. And the African maps were one big blank in the middle with no towns or mountains or rivers. In fact, in the old time,

> So, geographers, in Africa maps,
> With savage pictures fill their gaps,
> And o'er unhabitable downs
> Place elephants for want of towns.

16

Moffat, speaking of Africa, said to Livingstone, "There is a vast plain to the north where I have sometimes seen, in the morning sun, the smoke of a thousand villages where no missionary has ever been."

His imagination fired by this picture, Livingstone replied, "I will go at once to Africa."

The directors of the London Missionary Society agreed. He traveled from London through the November days to Scotland—to Blantyre—home. He could spend only one night there before he sailed from Glasgow on the long voyage to Africa.

"Let us sit up all night," said David.

"No," said his mother, who had so often made him as a boy close his books at midnight and go to bed, "you must rest."

At five o'clock on that next morning, November 17, 1840, the family got up. His mother put the kettle on the fire and made coffee. David took the Book and read in the One Hundred and Twenty-first Psalm to cheer his mother and father as they would be thinking of him in Africa:

> The sun shall not smite thee by day,
>   Nor the moon by night. . . .
> Jehovah will keep thy going out and thy coming in
> From this time forth and for evermore.

His sisters and his mother kissed him. His father, dressed in his best, started out and walked all the way

17

to Glasgow with David. On the Broomielaw quay father and son said good-by.

The father turned back to Blantyre; the son walked firmly up the gangway on board ship. They never saw each other again.

PART II

3 : Under the Lion's Paw

It was midnight on board the *George*. The moon hung high in the clear sky over the tropical sea. The long roll of the Atlantic Ocean made the ship's masts swing to and fro across the moon's face.

A cool night breeze after the blazing heat of the day refreshed two men who sat before some strange-looking instruments. One was the master of the *George*, Captain Donaldson; the other was David Livingstone. David was finding out from Captain Donaldson how to discover exactly where his ship was on the pathless ocean, by looking at the moon and stars and consulting those curious brass instruments and then working out sums.

"But why do you need to know all this?" the captain asked Livingstone. "You are not going to be a sailor. You are going to Africa to be a missionary—a man with a house and a garden and a church. The Africans with whom you live will tell you how to find your way."

To such a question Livingstone replied:

"Moffat told me of a great plain where he saw the smoke of a thousand villages and no white man had been there—and north of that is desert, and north of the desert no man knows. It may be that I shall go where no white man has gone. In that trackless desert and in the forest I should be as a ship in the pathless sea, unless I knew how to tell my path with such instruments as these—and those stars."

They sailed on always southward across the equator, Livingstone learning as he went.

"Algoa," cried the sailors on the *George* as the ship, after calling at Cape Town and rounding the Cape of Good Hope, came in view of Algoa Bay, where the Atlantic ends and the Indian Ocean begins. Here Livingstone landed and started inland. For three months he had rolled in the ship on the ocean. Now for seven hundred miles he was to jolt over the veld with African companions in a great ox wagon or ride on horseback.

He enjoyed the journey like a boy going on his first

camping holiday, though it was full of unexpected difficulties and provoking accidents. The creaking wagon, drawn by a long team of great oxen, toiled up the highlands of South Africa, over rough mountains, where often they could hardly move along, and down to the Orange River. In the ford there the great wagon stuck fast; the oxen got into disorder, some with their heads to the wagon where their tails ought to have been and others twisting and rolling as though they wanted to turn the wagon upside down. At last, after much shouting and cracking of whips, they were straightened out, started again, and toiled up the opposite bank of the river.

Sometimes the travelers had to urge the tired oxen on to do an extra hour's hard pulling. For, whatever happened, they must trek each day across the rocky veld far enough to reach some stream or water pit. At last one would shout, "A *vlei!*" (a large water pool), and the thirsty oxen would hurry on as they sniffed the water.

Then the order would be given to outspan and go into camp for the night. The men rushed to the oxen to unyoke them. One went off among the bushes in search of dry wood, while another started a small fire on which the wood was thrown. The blaze leaped up and licked with its flame the great kettle of water that was slung over it. A piece of one of the springboks (antelopes) that had been shot during the day was

23

hung over the red, glowing sticks of the fire, and in less than half an hour, as the sun set and the cold African night followed the blazing day, the travelers were sipping hot coffee and quite ready for their evening meal.

Yarns were told around the campfire, with talk of the adventures of the day that had gone and the plans for tomorrow, till, tired and sleepy, Livingstone and his companions would lie down for the night—he on the *kartel* (bed) in the wagon and the men in their blankets on the ground.

Early in the cool morning, after a hot pannikin of delicious coffee, the oxen would be inspanned and the wagon rolled onward. For four or five hours the oxen would tug at the yokes, till, when the sun blazed in mid-sky, they all stopped for a rest. A meal, quickly cooked, was eaten in the shade of the wagon. Then they would start again and creak and jolt across the wide rolling veld till the cry "Water" was again the signal to outspan for the night.

At last they rolled along to Kuruman, where Robert Moffat lived when in Africa. At this time he was still at home in England on furlough. Kuruman, once a lonely, bare, and scrubby spot, had been made a pleasant place with fruit trees, vines, and gardens.

Two miles away, at the foot of a bare hillside, a fountain of water bursts out of the dry rock, pouring down a rough, narrow valley in a stream that flows through

24

Kuruman. The missionaries had dug a trench the entire distance to bring the water to their houses and help in watering their gardens. Moffat himself, before he became a missionary, had been a working gardener at High Leigh in Cheshire, and he had used his skill as a gardener to make Kuruman more fruitful and beautiful than ever.

Livingstone gave his tired oxen only just sufficient time to rest after their tramp of seven hundred miles to Kuruman, which was then the pioneer station of the London Missionary Society in Africa. He could not get out of his mind "the plain of a thousand villages." Livingstone wished to find a place for settling two hundred and fifty miles farther north than any missionary had ever worked. This was the first journey in which he had the experience of eating the tough flesh of the rhinoceros for supper.

One morning on this journey, Livingstone, having left a large village, went some twelve miles on his day's course. He stopped the oxen for rest, and, looking back, saw a little African girl about eleven years old run up and sit down right underneath the wagon. She had no father or mother or sisters and had been taken by another family to be sold as a wife when she should grow old enough. She hated being a little slave, and she had seen the strong, kind face of Dr. Livingstone as he had healed men in the village where she lived. She

25

had run away to him and confidently asked him to protect her.

The missionary-doctor-traveler gave her some food and was glad to see her happier. But soon he heard her sobbing as though her heart would break. A man had come after her with a gun. She snatched off her beads and held them out to the man, begging him to take them and go away while a young native convert, named Pomare, jumped up to help defend her. He was the son of a chief and soon made the man with the gun go back home again.

Livingstone took the little girl and hid her in the most secret corner of his wagon. And he said, "Though fifty men come for her they will not find her."

The numerous tribes who lived in the part of Africa where Livingstone was now traveling called themselves by the names of animals. The people at Lepelole, where Livingstone went from Kuruman, called themselves the Bakwena, or the People of the Crocodile. *Ba* always means people. Chief Bubi ruled over them.

Livingstone stayed in their village for six months without seeing any man who could speak English. In this way he learned to speak the language of the Bakwena and learned all about their lives in their huts. He saw how much the hard-working women had to do while the men were out hunting. He discovered that they thought it shameful for even girls to cry. When he was taking a thorn out of a girl's foot, her mother said, "Now you are a woman, and a woman does not cry."

He saw the plump, brown, curly-headed younger ones tumbling and rolling in the sand at their play or sitting round playing cat's cradle or out among the bushes setting bird traps. The Bakwena were brave, but they were also cruel. He saw how much happier both the children and older people would be if they would stop the cruel fighting of one tribe with another.

They all lived in terror of the power of the sorcerers, men who use "magic spells" and gestures to terrify the African so that he actually dies because he believes that a demon-spirit is destroying him. Livingstone saw that the best way to free the people from the fear of the sorcerer and of demons was to teach them that there is one Father—God—who cares for them.

This village of Lepelole was not very far from the great Kalahari Desert. Though there was a stream near the village, there was very little rain.

In Africa the "witch doctor," as he is called, uses "magic," but generally he wields his powers in order to help his tribe, not—as the sorcerer does—to harm or kill men. The Bakwena witch doctor, who called himself a rain maker, tried to make the rain come by many spells—but he could not. Livingstone told the chief that *he* would bring water to their gardens.

27

They had only one spade, and that was without a handle, but Livingstone and the men—including the rain maker!—all set to work and dug out a little canal, through which the water ran from the stream in and out among the gardens. Then the vegetables all began to grow. The witch doctor laughed very much at the way the "foreigner's" cleverness had done what his own magic could not work.

Although these witch doctors generally use their powers to help their tribe, nevertheless, as we shall see later, they are the cause of many deaths. They test whether an accused criminal is guilty or not by a poison test, which, more often than not, kills the accused.

When Livingstone had dug the canal for the People of the Crocodile and had built a part of a new house, he took a long trip still farther north across a part of the Kalahari Desert.

One day he walked into the village of a tribe, the Bakaa. He was told to be careful, for they had just murdered a traveling trader. Yet quite fearlessly Livingstone went among these men, sat down with them, ate part of their porridge, and then calmly lay down and slept in the very presence of these murderers. They did not lay a hand on him.

As he traveled on this journey, Livingstone's ox wagon was often besieged by blind, lame, and sick people asking the good white doctor to heal them.

Some had come more than one hundred miles to be healed. Livingstone gained his great power over the lives of the Africans, not by kicks or whips, as many white men have tried to do, but by being brave in danger, kind to them in sickness, and laughing with them as he taught them to water their gardens. Yet he was very firm and serious when he pointed out to them the wrong in their lives and told them about Jesus who would help them be stronger.

It made them listen to his words, also, when they found that he could walk, ride, shoot game, and swim as well as and often better than they could. One day he was trudging along with his African companions on the trip among the tribes on the edge of the Kalahari Desert. They were walking because the oxen were ill. He heard one of the men say to the others quietly, "He is not strong. He is quite slim and only looks stout because he puts himself into those bags. He will soon give out."

This roused Livingtone's Highland blood. All his boyhood walks on the Scottish hills helped him now, for he was able to walk the men at the top of their speed for day after day up the great hills and round the valleys of the Bakaa Mountains till his African companions marveled and begged to be allowed to go more slowly.

While Livingstone was wandering among these tribes,

a cruel and powerful African chief drove his old friends, the People of the Crocodile, right away from Lepelole, where he had started his mission house and dug his canal. He made up his mind that he must go to another people, the Bakhatla, or the People of the Monkey.

When Livingstone asked the Bakhatla chief if he would like him to come and be his missionary, the chief threw up his hands in delight and said, "Oh, I shall dance if you do. I shall collect all my people to hoe a garden for you!"

Before he settled down in the village of this chief, Livingstone took another journey. He traveled four hundred miles, riding, for the first time, on the back of a great ox. The skin of the pack ox is very loose and rolls about. The ox also has very long horns, which, when it swings its head to knock away the flies, are likely to punch into the waist of the rider.

At night Livingstone would have his ox tied up, and then he would sit with the people around the village fire listening to the hero legends of the Africans. Then he would tell true stories about Jesus in Bethlehem and Galilee and upon the cross.

One day, as he was walking down a steep pass among the mountains, he was so taken up with answering the questions that his African companions asked him that he stumbled and broke his finger against a rock. Some days later, when the finger was getting better, he was awakened in the middle of the night by the terrific roar of a lion. Looking out, he seized his revolver and fired it at the great beast. The lion fled, but the recoil of the revolver broke Livingstone's finger again. His native companions, seeing the blood flowing, said, "You have hurt yourself, but you have saved us. From this time we will be only yours."

After Livingstone returned from this journey, he went with three English hunters to live, as he had promised, among the People of the Monkey. These Bakhatla lived among rivers and mountains, a fortnight's travel north of Kuruman. The place was called Mabotsa, which means "marriage feast." It was in a lovely valley, with a semicircle of big hills behind.

The night was often made terrible at Mabotsa by the roar of lions, sounding among the hills like thunder. Livingstone was teaching the Bakhatla to dig canals for their gardens when the work was stopped by the ferocious attacks of these lions. One of them had leaped among the herds in the open day and had killed some cows. The excited and terrified villagers of Mabotsa gathered in groups to talk about the extraordinary thing that had happened.

"We are bewitched," they said. "Who ever saw the lion, the lord of the night, kill our cattle by day?" They were so terrified that, although they marched out to kill the lions, they went shaking with fear. Since cowards never conquer, the Mabotsa people came back with not a single slain lion.

They were ashamed, yet trembled at the thought of trying again to kill the lions. Some days passed, and once more a lion, roaring with rage, sprang among the sheep and slew nine in broad daylight on the hill opposite Livingstone's house.

Livingstone was named David after the shepherd boy who smote the lion that had done harm among his herds. He now lived up to the name. He knew that, if this one lion were killed, the rest would leave that part of the country.

The lions were on a little hill covered with trees. The People of the Monkey closed round this hill. Livingstone and a native schoolmaster, named Mebalwe, waited with guns. They saw one of the lions sitting on a piece of rock. Mebalwe fired. The ball struck the rock, and the lion "bit at the spot struck, as a dog bites at a stick or stone thrown at him." Then leaping away, it broke through the circle of men and escaped unhurt. Two other lions escaped in this way. The Bakhatla, believing that they were bewitched, feared to throw their spears. So the people all started to go home.

"In going round the end of the hill, however," Livingstone tells us, "I saw one of the beasts sitting on a piece of rock as before, but this time he had a little bush in front. Being about thirty yards off, I took a good aim at his body through the bush and fired both barrels into it.

"The men then called out, 'He is shot! He is shot!' . . . I saw a lion's tail erected in anger behind the bush and, turning to the people, said, 'Stop a little till I load again.' When in the act of ramming down the bullet, I heard a shout. Starting and looking half round, I saw the lion just in the act of springing upon me. I was upon a little height; he caught my shoulder as he sprang, and we both came to the ground below together.

"Growling horribly close to my ear, he shook me as a terrier does a rat. The shock produced a stupor similar to that which a mouse must feel after the first shake of a cat. It caused a sort of dreaminess, in which there was no sense of pain nor feeling of terror.

"Turning round to relieve myself of the weight, as he had one paw on the back of my head, I saw his eyes directed to Mebalwe, who was trying to shoot him, at a distance of ten or fifteen yards. His gun missed fire in both barrels; the lion immediately left me and, attacking Mebalwe, bit his thigh. Another man, whose life I had saved before, after he had been tossed by a buffalo, attempted to spear the lion while he was biting Mebalwe. He left Mebalwe and caught this man by the shoulder, but at that moment the bullets he had received took effect, and he fell down dead."

The bone at the top of Livingstone's left arm was crunched into splinters, and there were eleven toothmarks on his arm. The People of the Monkey said that this was the largest lion they had ever seen. They thought he had been charmed by a sorcerer of another tribe so that he could kill them. So they built a great bonfire over the dead lion to burn out the charm.

4 : *The Queen of the Wagon*

All trembling with fear, a crowd of shining, naked brown pupils came to school for the first time. They were afraid because they had been told by their mothers that the white man would bite them. The mothers were wrong, for the schoolmaster was as kind as he was strong. The school was at Mabotsa, and the master was Livingstone.

So the children, with wide wondering eyes rolling with fright and curiosity, tried to hide behind one another when they saw their white schoolmaster with his wounded arm. The first day they would not have come to school, but the Bakhatla chief and Mebalwe had said that they must. The next day they wanted to come because they liked it.

There were no desks, no maps, and no pictures. All the earth was a playground, but the boldest boy would not go far into the woods. For however interesting it is to read of lion adventures, it is not so pleasant to know that one may be lurking unseen in a thicket ten yards away, crouching ready to spring, and with no bars between you and him.

While his arm was healing, Livingstone traveled back to Kuruman and went one hundred and fifty miles farther to meet Robert Moffat, who was coming back from England to his work as a missionary at Kuruman. When Livingstone rode up to the wagon, he saw sitting beside Mrs. Moffat her eldest daughter, Mary.

David and Mary soon fell in love, and under the great almond tree at Kuruman, which still throws out its blossoms, they became engaged. After they were married they went back together to live at Mabotsa—which, you remember, means a "marriage feast." There Mary began to teach in the African school.

David and Mary lived in a little stone and brick house that Livingstone and his helpers had built with their own hands. Livingstone had to do most of the building himself because the Bakhatla were so used to building round huts that they could not lay the stones and bricks in straight lines! He also had to make the bricks himself. The doors and the windows he and his helpers made from the trees standing in the forest. Livingstone said, "Every brick and every stick was put square by my own right hand."

He and Mary together had to churn their own butter in a jar, mold their own candles, and make their own soap with the ash of plants, for the nearest store was hundreds of miles away.

"My wife is maid-of-all-work, and I am Jack-of-all-trades," said Livingstone.

Because the sun in Africa is terribly hot in the middle of the day, they would get up early in the morning and be eating breakfast by six o'clock. At about eight they would go to the school, where they would find men, women, and children waiting to be taught, for not even the older Bakhatla knew how to read or write. School would be over by eleven o'clock, when Livingstone would dig in the garden or do some carpentry. Sometimes he worked with hammer and anvil as a blacksmith, making some tool or mending a kitchen kettle for his wife, who was at work in the house.

After dinner and an hour's rest in the hottest part of the day, Mary would go off to her school, where she would find a hundred children ready to cluster round her and be taught—for now they loved her and the school very much. She also taught the older girls how to sew. In the afternoon and evening Livingstone would treat those who were sick. As soon as the cows were milked, he would gather the men and women together and hold a service under the stars to worship God and speak about his love.

Another missionary came to Mabotsa. And after a while Livingstone and his wife made up their minds to move still farther on into a place where no missionary was at work. The Bakhatla came round the wagon when it was all ready to start and begged Livingstone not to leave them. They said, "Do stay, and we will build another house for you."

But Livingstone the Pathfinder was always a pioneer, eager to push forward. So with Mrs. Livingstone as "Queen of the Wagon," the oxen strained at the yokes, the driver cracked his whip, and the great wagon rolled on away from the Bakhatla, the People of the Monkey, for forty miles northward.

When they came to Chonuane (a village of the People of the Crocodile, the Bakwena), the chief, Sechele, welcomed them with delight. Livingstone at Chonuane built another house, and he and Mary began to teach the children in Sechele's village and to live very much as they had done at Mabotsa. Sechele did not know how to read, nor had he even seen a book before, but he was so bright that he learned the whole alphabet in one day.

He wanted all the people in his tribe to become Christians and suggested to Livingstone that the best way would be for Sechele, as chief, to give orders for them all to be thrashed with great whips made of rhinoceros hide till they said they would worship Jesus. It took Livingstone some time to show Sechele that Jesus wants people to come to him not through fear but because they love him.

One day these people in Chonuane, all smiles and wide-open eyes, were talking about something that they had never seen before in all their lives. It was Mary and David Livingstone's baby son, who was named Robert for his grandfather Robert Moffat. And— as the Africans call mothers after their sons—Mrs. Livingstone was called Ma-Robert.

One day this white baby and all the other children in Chonuane found themselves being taken out of their homes and carried away by their mothers to new homes. This happened because the sun went on shining day after day, week after week, and month after month with not a drop of rain. It was so hot and blistering that if you put a beetle on the sand in the sun he was scorched to death in a few minutes.

The people could not live without water so Livingstone made up his mind to move on again in order to find a better place for them. This time he planned to go to the rocky land at Kolobeng by the side of a river.

The very next day after he had told them that he must go, Livingstone found all the people rushing about as busy as ants, for they had made up their minds that they could not live without Livingstone, their white protector and teacher and friend. So they left their old village and went with him to build a new one at Kolobeng.

The country around Kolobeng was full of wild beasts that even came into the village. Livingstone, standing at the front door of his own house, shot a rhinoceros and a buffalo.

At Kolobeng Livingstone helped the people to make the water run out of the river into little ditches through their gardens. In addition, he and Ma-Robert taught the children of the village in a school that Chief Sechele built for them.

One evening, when the work of the day was done and the people were getting ready for rest, an African came rushing into the village, panting for breath and with terror on his face. He ran to Livingstone and told him breathlessly how a party of hunters about ten miles away in the forest had suddenly been startled by a black rhinoceros. The beast had rushed in fury at the wagon and had driven his horn—which can kill even an elephant—into the driver. The messenger had run every step of the way to fetch Dr. Livingstone.

The doctor at once began to harness his horse so

that he might ride with his medicine to help save the wounded man's life.

"No, you must not go," said his friends. "The forest is full of danger; you know that there are the lion, the rhinoceros, and other wild beasts prowling in it for prey at night."

Livingstone felt that he must—as a follower of Jesus, who healed men—go to help the wounded driver. He rode that night ten miles of perilous journey, at every step of which some beast might have sprung out upon him. When he reached the spot, the wagon had gone. The wounded man was dead, and Livingstone had to ride back home through the dark forest.

Time went on, and two more babies were added to the little family at Kolobeng. They kept Ma-Robert company while their father was away on long journeys.

Livingstone had heard reports of a great lake that lay across the Kalahari Desert hundreds of miles northward. Chief Sechele had told him that no white man could possibly cross the desert. But Livingstone had made up his mind that the missionaries must go on and on until the whole of mysterious Africa was opened up. Many people said that it was all one enormous desert from the Sahara on the north to the Kalahari on the south. He felt sure that it was not so.

Just then a young chief named Lechulatebe, who

lived near this unknown lake and had heard of Livingstone, sent messengers right across the desert asking him to come to the lake. The messengers said that Lechulatebe was so great a chief that he made even his cattle pens of elephant tusks.

Livingstone, with two great travelers named Murray and Oswell, who wished to go with him, took ox wagons and started north over the wooded hills and down to the dried up bed of an ancient river. Here the country was flat with thorny trees. Farther on, in a beautiful place of deep wells, they saw many leaping antelopes, chattering monkeys, and cackling guinea-fowl.

The land got drier and sandier, and as they struck into the desert, the wheels sank deep into the soft white sand, through which the thirsty oxen could hardly drag the wagons. In this desert country, although there are few wells and no rivers, Livingstone saw great herds of swift running antelopes and flocks of ostriches, while the lion roared in the deep grass and the hyena and the jackal howled under the moon among prickly shrubs.

The plants in the desert live by sending roots deep down into the sand to the water underneath. The antelopes feed on the grass and on the wonderful roots—like great turnips, as big as a boy's head—that grow about two feet under the surface and are full of cool and delicious juice.

One evening during this journey Livingstone and his

party, burning with thirst, came to a village of the little Bushmen living in the desert. They are a yellowish brown hunting people, and their language is nearly all clicks.

Some travelers, when they came very thirsty to a Bushman village and saw no wells at all, ordered the people to give them water. And when the Bushmen said, "We have no water," the travelers threatened to kill the Bushmen. This resulted in the Bushmen firing poisoned arrows at the travelers and killing them.

But when Livingstone reached the Bushman village, he sat down quietly with his followers and in a friendly manner let them know that he was thirsty. Soon women came to him, bringing great ostrich eggshells full of water.

How the Bushwomen got water into these eggshells when there was no rain and no wells and no river, and how they hid the shells so that no one could find them even if they searched every hut in the village had puzzled many people.

This is the explanation. Deep down under the ancient dried up river beds there flows through the sand a slow stream of water. The Bushwomen dig a deep hole, put a bunch of grass at the bottom, stand a hollow reed in the hole, and then fill it up with sand. They then suck the water up the reed (the grass at the bottom filtering it) and pour it into the empty ostrich eggshells.

43

When a shell is full, they plug up the hole with grass. When they have filled many shells, they carry them back to their villages, dig a hole, and bury the shells in the cool earth. Sometimes, when strangers are coming, they light their village fire on the earth over the very spot where the watershells are buried.

Livingstone and his friends traveled on, day after day, in the glare of the bright sun in a cloudless sky, often going for days without finding water. They came to no lake and wondered whether the stories that had been told to them were true. Suddenly they saw, through a beautiful blue haze, dancing wavelets and the shadow of trees. Oswell, the hunter, threw his hat into the air and cheered; the animals rushed down to drink. But the Bushwoman who was then guiding them laughed. It was all a mirage, made by the dancing rays of the sun on the flat, salt covered sand of the desert. The lake was three hundred miles away!

It was not long, however, before they came to a slowly flowing river called the Zouga with beautifully wooded banks. The oxen tugged the wagons along the banks till they came to a strange tribe who never fought their enemies.

These Africans lived nearly all the time on the river in canoes, hollowed out of the trunks of single trees with an iron tool. If there was a bend in the tree, so there was in the canoe. They had fires in the canoes

44

and would go to sleep there saying, "On land you have the lions, serpents, hyenas, enemies—in your canoe in a bank of reeds you are safe."

Livingstone enjoyed traveling most of the way in a swift canoe instead of in the ox wagon, which jolted along the bank. As the Africans paddled along, with the waters of the Zouga rippling against the gliding sides of the canoes, they came to another river running from the north into the Zouga. It is called the Tamunak'le.

"Whence does that river come?" asked Livingstone as they paused and the water dripped from the paddles into the stream.

"Oh," said the Africans, "it flows from a country full of rivers—so many that no one can tell their number—and full of large trees!"

This answer excited Livingstone. Nearly everybody in England and America then believed that most of Africa was sandy desert. But if what these men said was true, there was not only a desert but also a wonderful forest and mountain country, with millions of people in it. It would be possible for missionaries to go among them in canoes along the many rivers. If Livingstone could find this was true, he would open the mightiest unknown land in the whole world. It is no wonder that he was excited and enthusiastic.

A few days later, on August 1, 1849, they saw the shining waters of Lake Ngami stretching far away beyond their sight. It had never been seen by white men before. Lake Ngami was Livingstone's first great discovery. But his brain was full of what lay beyond even those waters—the country "full of rivers—so many that no one can tell their number—and full of large trees."

Livingstone wanted to go immediately into the country north of the river Zouga. But Chief Lechulatebe, who had asked him to come as far as the lake, did not want him to go away beyond. He would not help Livingstone, who therefore tried with all his might to bind together a raft in the river on which to cross with his wagons and oxen. But the wood was all rotten and would not make a raft. It gave Livingstone a cold shiver afterwards to find that the river in which he had been working waist-deep for hours was full of crocodiles!

He went back across the fringes of the Kalahari Desert, home to Kolobeng. There was great excitement among his children, Robert, Agnes, and Thomas, when he said, "You must all come with me next time."

But we do not know what their mother thought about crossing the thirsty desert as Queen of the Wagon with three little children.

5 : *African Journeys*

Davvid Livingstone kept the promise that he had made to his children. He packed them into the wagon the following year with Ma-Robert, and they started out.

They looked out of the wagon with wonder as they saw antelopes galloping away through the bushes and grass, and the little Bushmen with their bows and arrows hunting game. Their eyes were dazzled by the sunlight on the yellow sand, and they were sorry for the oxen as they strained at the yokes, trying to draw the great wagon across the desert. Day after day they went on. As they drew near to the other edge of the Kalahari Desert, they saw zebras and buffaloes running up from the water holes as the wagon rolled nearer and nearer.

At last they reached the great river Zouga, where the children pointed to the dark Bakoba paddling in their tree-trunk canoes. Robert, the eldest child, wanted to go out on the river in one of them.

The elephants, with mighty gurglings and splashings, came down to drink at the river. The children saw them draw the water up their trunks with a snort and then squirt it out in a fountain all over their great bodies, squealing with delight as they felt the cool water splashing and running down their sides.

Sometimes Ma-Robert and the children had a shock when they saw an ox in the team suddenly fall through what looked like solid earth and disappear into a pit. These pits were dug by the Bakoba to catch animals as they came down to drink. If a baby elephant fell into one of these pits, his big mother would curl her trunk round him and tug and pull until she had drawn him back to safety once more.

Often the Livingstones had to stop quite a long time in one place while the men cut down trees to clear a path for the wagon. Then they had to go round by a way that Dr. Livingstone did not know in order to avoid the banks of the river at certain places where the dreaded tsetse fly was found. This fly, a little larger than a house fly, kills oxen, cattle, and horses with its bite and causes sleeping sickness in humans. At last, with shouts of joy, the children came in sight of the lake that their father had discovered. They were soon paddling and playing in it like ducklings, while Livingstone and Ma-Robert stood by laughing at them as they splashed in the clear waters of Lake Ngami.

Livingstone wished to press farther on, to see the powerful chief of the Makololo, whose name was Sebituane, but two of the children and others of the party became ill with a fever. He hurried back to the drier, healthier air of the desert, and from there on home to Kolobeng.

There a baby sister was born, "a sweet little girl with blue eyes." But just at that time many of the African children of Kolobeng were ill, and the Livingstones' new daughter caught the sickness, which ended her life when she was only six weeks old, not long before Christmas in 1850.

The children went again on the strange journey through the desert up to the country of forest and rivers the next April. Mr. Oswell, the hunter, was with them this time, and he went on with his men in advance to dig wells so that when Ma-Robert got there with her children she would find plenty of water for them. But they came to a part of the desert that was drier than they had ever seen it before, and there was no water even under the sand. Everything was so dry and lifeless that for three whole days they did not see a single insect or hear a bird chirp. Their faithful guide, a clever little Bushman named Shobo, lost his way in the trackless wilderness. It would be hard to tell who among the members of the expedition suffered the most.

For four awful days the entire party was absolutely without water. One of the servants had spilled the water that had been kept in the wagons. The children moaned and cried with the burning thirst, and Livingstone felt how terrible it was that he had brought them to this suffering. He even wished that Ma-Robert would blame him. She did not say a word of reproach, but it hurt him all the more to see the tears in her eyes and to know the dark fears that filled her heart as she realized the increasing dangers of their situation.

On the afternoon of the fifth day one of their men who had gone ahead came back shouting and carrying with him some water from a spring that he had found. The children drank the cool water with gulps of delight while the mother and father could look into one another's eyes again without seeing the dread that had been there.

At last, after they had gone along the Zouga and up the Tamunak'le, which flows into it from the north, they came to the home of the great Sebituane, head of the

Makololo. He was a warlike chief, who knew how to teach people to love him as well as to make his enemies fear him.

Sebituane could run more swiftly than any other man in his tribe. Before a battle, in order to make the cowards among his men more brave, he would take up his battle-ax and, feeling its edge with his thumb, shout out, "Aha! it is sharp, and whoever turns his back on the enemy will feel its edge."

Sebituane became very friendly with Livingstone at once. He promised to choose a place where Livingstone could build a house. But in only a few weeks Sebituane was taken ill. He became worse and worse till it was clear that he could not recover. His last words were to tell Livingstone to take his newly born son to Maunku—one of Sebituane's wives—who would give him some milk.

His daughter Mamochisane ruled in his place, and she, too, proved to be friendly to Livingstone and his work.

Livingstone left his wife and children at the village while he and Mr. Oswell went northeast, through the town of Linyanti. On August 3, 1851, they found a new, lovely river. It was so broad that when they crossed it the waves "made the canoe roll beautifully." They were so excited and delighted that all they could do was to say to one another, "How glorious! How magnificent!

How beautiful!" It was only afterwards that they discovered that this river was the great Zambezi, which flows over Victoria Falls and finally empties into the Indian Ocean.

Livingstone felt he simply must find a path to the east or west coast of Africa along which the missionaries and traders might come into Central Africa. Yet he knew now, as he saw his children taken ill again and again with fever, that he must not keep them traveling in this country.

What was he to do? He decided that they must go home to England with their mother for two years while he found the path to the coast. Then he could settle in some healthful spot, and they could all, he thought, come back again.

So he took them back to their old home at Kolobeng. Imagine their surprise when they found that all the people, with Chief Sechele, had gone away. The Boers had driven them off, shooting at them with guns, so as to stop Livingstone's plans. Today some of the great-grandchildren of the very Boers who opposed Livingstone are themselves working hard as missionaries in South Africa.

Livingstone was more certain than ever that he must find a way into the heart of Africa farther north where the Boers could not spoil the work. He said, "I will go anywhere, provided it be forward."

Dr. Livingstone, Ma-Robert, and the children now turned their faces back toward the Cape. They went to see their grandfather, Robert Moffat, at Kuruman and then on and on to the very southern tip of Africa at the Cape of Good Hope.

There the mother took her four children, Robert and Agnes, Thomas and the new baby, William Oswell, on a ship that sailed away to England. How their father felt at this parting from his family we can guess from his letter to his little daughter, who was then between four and five years old:

CAPE TOWN
18*th* May, 1852

MY DEAR AGNES:

This is your own little letter. Mamma will read it to you and you will hear her just as if I were speaking to you, for the words which I write are those which she will read.

I am still at Cape Town. You know you left me there when you all went into the big ship and sailed away. Well, I shall leave Cape Town soon. Malatsi has gone for the oxen, and then I shall go away back to Sebituane's country, and see Seipone and Meriye, who gave you the beads and fed you with milk and honey.

I shall not see you again for a long time, and I am very sorry. I have no Nannie now. I have given you back to Jesus, your Friend—your Papa who is in heaven. He is above you, but he is always near you. When we ask things from him, that is praying to him; and if you do or say a naughty thing ask him to pardon you, and bless you, and make you one of his children.

Love Jesus much, for he loves you and he came and died for you. Oh, how good Jesus is! I love him, and I shall love him as long as I live. You must love him, too, and you must love your brothers and Mamma, and never tease them or be naughty, for Jesus does not like to see naughtiness. Good-by, my dear Nannie.

D. LIVINGSTONE

PART III

6 : The Pathfinder

Livingstone wrote to Ma-Robert as well as to Agnes. He said to his wife:

MY DEAREST MARY:

How I miss you now and the dear children! . . . I see no face now to be compared with the sunburnt one which has so often greeted me with its kind looks. . . . Take the children all around you and kiss them for me. Tell them I have left them for the love of Jesus, and they must love him, too, and avoid sin, for that displeases Jesus. I shall be delighted to hear of you all safe in England. . . .

Feeling very lonely, he got into his ox wagon and started back on the long trail again. When he got to

Kuruman, he heard from Moffat of the terrible thing that had happened at his home at Kolobeng while he had been away in the north.

The Boers had not only shot many of Sechele's people and driven the chief away, but they had ruined Livingstone's house, carried away all his furniture for themselves, and torn up all the manuscript diaries in which he had told the story of his early travels and adventures.

Sechele's wife had escaped, with her baby, and she fled to Kuruman to tell Mrs. Moffat.

"How did you manage to get away without being captured?" asked Mrs. Moffat.

Then Masebele, the wife of Sechele, told of her hairbreadth escape.

"I hid," she said, "in a cleft in the rock, with my baby. And the Boers came closer and closer, shooting with their guns. They came till they were on the rock just over my head. I could see the muzzles of the guns above the cleft as they fired. The baby began to scream, and I felt sure that they would hear and capture us, but I took off these armlets and gave them to Baby to play with. That kept Baby quiet, and the Boers passed on without finding us."

Livingstone was both sad and angry when he heard how his friends the People of the Crocodile at Kolobeng had been treated and robbed of their cattle and how all his medicines had been destroyed. But bravely he made jokes about his own house being destroyed and his furniture taken off, saying that it set him free for traveling. He wrote home to his wife:

We shall move more easily now that we are lightened of our furniture. They have taken away our sofa. I never had a good rest on it. Well, they can't have taken away all the stones. We shall have a seat in spite of them, and that, too, with a merry heart, which doeth good like a medicine.

The Boers have made up their minds to close the country. I am determined to open it. Time will show who will win.

I will open a path through the country, or—PERISH.

Soon Livingstone was traveling over the Kalahari Desert again, on another of those hard wagon journeys that he enjoyed so much. He once said that they were just one long picnic, which all would enjoy who were not too dainty about food and who delighted in the open air. In this "wild, healthful, gypsy life," as he went north, he saw many wonders and had many hardships and adventures. He saw flocks of ostriches with black, white, and brown feathers. When they were running in terror, they took strides fourteen feet long. He heard the ostriches roaring in the day with a sound just like the lions roaring at night. He killed a huge python that was twice as long as a man, as thick as a man's leg, and lifted its head five feet high.

Again and again lions, with their tawny manes showing in the moonlight, came up close to the camp at night and roared to frighten the oxen, but they were afraid of the campfire.

When the men reached the Chobe River, it was in flood as it was at that time every year. They could not cross with the wagons, for they had no raft. But in one wagon was a pontoon—a kind of small boat raft. So, leaving the wagons, they paddled across to a plain ankle-deep in water and knee-deep in grass. They shot a water antelope, waded to a group of trees on drier ground and collected wood, made "a glorious fire," cooked the antelope, and slept in safety.

In the morning they climbed to the top of the highest trees. From the treetops they saw some islands that looked as though they might furnish a means of crossing the river. So they climbed down again and tried to wade to the islands.

A rough grass among the reeds cut their hands and clothes as they waded through the water. The climbing convolvulus bound the reeds together so that they could get through only by leaning against the reeds till they all went flat. The knees of Livingstone's trousers were cut through, so he tore his handkerchief in two and bound his knees with that.

They searched about till they found a spot where a hippopotamus had pushed a way through with his huge head. But the water, in which snakes and otters were swimming, was so deep that no one could walk across.

They had to go back, tired out, and they lay down close to the reeds in an old hut, with mosquitoes buzzing and biting.

It looked as though Livingstone would either have to turn back or leave his wagons. But he refused, now as always, to give up till he had tried again and again to push through obstacles.

So in the morning he and his men went back for the pontoon and paddled on it across the deep river. In the middle of the river a huge hippopotamus suddenly came up close to them like a volcanic island. They had passed over him. The wave that he made rocked the pontoon and made it glide quickly away from him.

They paddled on from noon till sunset, but no opening could they find in the reeds; then, just before the swift African night came on, they discovered, on the north bank, a Makololo village, with people in it whom Livingstone had met on his last journey. The Makololo looked at him with astonished eyes as though they had seen a ghost. They said, "He has dropped among us from the clouds, yet came riding on the back of a hippopotamus. We Makololo thought no one could cross the Chobe without our knowledge, but here he drops among us like a bird."

Livingstone was now among good friends. The Makololo paddled him back across the Chobe in canoes, took his wagons to pieces, and carried them across on the canoes tied together. They made the oxen swim across the river, "diving among them more like alligators than men."

They then went on to Linyanti, the capital village of the Makololo. All the six thousand Makololo in Linyanti rushed out to see Livingstone's wagons. They had never seen such things before. The old herald leaped about with excitement at the sight of Livingstone and roared at the top of his voice, "Don't I see the comrade of Sebituane? Don't I see the father of Sekeletu?"

Sebituane, the brave and swift running, had died. Sekeletu, his son, who was only eighteen years old, was chief in his place since Sekeletu's sister, Mamochisane, did not want to be chief. Young Sekeletu soon became very fond of Livingstone, whom he called "my new father."

"Your coffee," he said to Livingstone, "tastes nicer than that of the traders because they like my ivory and you like me."

One day Livingstone and Sekeletu, riding on oxen, started off from Linyanti at the head of a long line of Makololo followers. The women and children stood watching the procession winding its way along the curving path. The strange headdresses of the line of dark figures nodded as the men marched behind Livingstone. One had tied on his head the tuft of white hairs from the end of the tail of an ox. Another was very proud of a great bunch of waving ostrich feathers. A third man looked very fierce wearing a lion's tawny mane.

Livingstone and Sekeletu, with their company, traveled till they came to a mighty river, more than a mile broad—the Zambezi. The men stood upright in a fleet of thirty-three canoes. Swiftly the boats flew along under the strokes of long eight-foot paddles, which were used as punting poles when the river was shallow. The hundred and sixty men, who were partly Makololo and partly of the Barotse tribe, kept beautiful time as the canoes skimmed over the water, sometimes dashing along and racing one another at the top of their speed.

When they came to cataracts and rapids, which no boat could pass and survive, Livingstone decided to turn back to Linyanti. As they returned down the river, the canoe men saw a group of African hunters on the river bank rush off in fear. Livingstone's men, who all their lives before they met him had been accustomed to plunder strangers, dashed up with shoutings and seized all the hunters' goods. Livingstone was vexed with them and sternly told them to put everything down on the ground and leave it. For though Livingstone was always kind to his African friends, he was very firm with them when they did wrong. They took notice when he was displeased with them. So these fierce warriors obeyed him at once and put back the plundered pots and pans and clothes.

Livingstone on this journey met some Arab slave traders. These men would take a whole village—men, women, and children—into slavery. They would handcuff the slaves and tie them together with forked poles fastened to their necks. Hundreds of the people would die on the road, and those who lived would be set to work in plantations under the lash of an overseer.

Livingstone hated this slave trading with a great and burning hatred. He soon began to make it one great aim of his life to sweep slave trading away from Africa. He told these Arabs how much better it was to let children grow up to comfort their own mothers than to carry them away and sell them to strange men across the sea.

When Livingstone and his friends got back to Linyanti, he thought of a daring plan. He wanted to stop these men from making slaves of the Africans and to end the horrible fighting and killing that he saw going on in the villages among all the African people.

His plan for helping to do away with all these evil things was to find a way from the center of Africa, where he now was, out to the coast. Up that new track, he thought, men could come to bring the story of the love of Jesus. Down that road the Africans could carry their ivory tusks, coffee, cotton, and other goods so that

64

true trade would take the place of the evil trade in human beings.

So Livingstone the Pathfinder set out once more on his quest. He had come to a decision from which nothing, whether beast, savage men, marsh, forest, fever, or the yearning for home, could turn him:

"I will open a path into the interior or perish."

7: By Canoe and Forest Track

When Livingstone told Sekeletu that he wished to find a way to the coast, the chief called a *picho*, which is similar to the American Indian powwow, to decide whether his men would help. The chief men of the village all gathered round while Sekeletu sat with Livingstone in the center as they listened to the discussion.

"Where is the white doctor taking you?" asked one old man. "He is throwing you away. Your garments already smell of blood."

But the others were in favor of going with "Nyaka,"

or "the doctor," as they called Livingstone. They lent him twenty-seven men to bear the luggage and help him. If Livingstone had been obliged, like most explorers, to pay for all his carriers, he could never have accomplished his exploring—for he had very little money. But his wonderful power of winning the trust of the Africans helped him to get good and faithful bearers—just for love.

So Livingstone and his twenty-seven African companions started off on their tremendous pathfinding. He left his wagons in charge of the Makololo at Linyanti. One man carried a tin box with some spare clothing in it. Another bore his case of medicines, a third his books —one of which was his Bible—and a fourth his picture projector. Others carried his small gypsy tent, a sheepskin mantle, and a horse rug, and some of the instruments that he learned to use when sailing on the *George* from Britain. No man ever traveled so perilous and long a journey with so little provision, but Livingstone believed that "brains and pluck" were the best traveling baggage.

Chief Sekeletu took them as far as the Chobe, a branch of the Zambezi, which was full of hippopotami. Some of the lonely ones, called "bachelors," were very ferocious. Livingstone saw a canoe that had been smashed to pieces by one "bachelor" hippopotamus while another chased some of his men, although they escaped. Sekeletu turned back when he saw Livingstone and his men safely on board their canoes. How fond he was of Livingstone is shown by the fact that he lent him his own canoe. And as they went along the river and called at the villages, Livingstone found that Sekeletu had sent orders on ahead, that "Nyaka must not be allowed to become hungry."

Their canoes glided swiftly down the Chobe to the place where it joins the great Zambezi. Paddling up the Zambezi toward its source to the left, they worked now against the stream, for the Zambezi flows southeastward across Africa and Livingstone was searching for a way to the west coast. He soon came to a big village of the Makololo called Sesheke. He stayed there for some days and preached often to some six hundred people on the high bank of the river under a camel thorn tree. At one of these services, Moriantsane, the chief, seeing some young fellows preparing to skin an animal instead of listening, stood up and hurled his staff at their heads to make them pay attention.

After leaving Sesheke, they traveled many days up the Zambezi.

Each morning Livingstone rose before five o'clock. While the white mist still hung over the water, one of the men lighted a wood fire and hung over it a kettle of water. Soon the rich aroma of coffee drew them all for a bracing drink from the pannikin.

The men quickly loaded the canoes and soon the most pleasant part of the day's journey began. Along the river Livingstone noticed birds of every kind. The tall fishing ibis sat on the end of an old tree stump shouting "Wa-wa-wa" as they passed. The little green parrots, with yellow shoulders, shrieked and chattered while the kingfishers flashed like lightning over the water. In the shallows a tall vermilion flamingo gazed down on the little fish, choosing the one that would best suit his taste.

As his canoe skimmed swiftly round a corner, he heard the crocodiles splash from the bank into the water while the quaint iguana reptiles, which had been sunning themselves on the branches over the stream, dropped like stones into the water—but not before the Barotse man in the bow of the canoe had with a swift, sure aim of his light javelin speared one for supper.

As he sat there in the canoe scanning the banks, nothing seemed to escape Livingstone's bright, fearless, blue-gray eyes. He noted everything from the tall palmyra treetops and the many-colored tangle of creeper and flower to the kind of soil through which the river ran. He saw, from the color of the water in the river, the soil that it had already drained.

He watched the habits of every creature from the huge hippopotamus down to a curious ant-eating insect that stands on its head to attract the ants and wags a feathery tail in which are hidden a pair of tweezers.

He reckoned the kind of crop that each part of the country could bear. He found his direction and guided his travel on the vast trackless continent by the stars. And, living for a year among men who were by nature filthy-mouthed, quarrelsome, vain, and violent, he remained clean, strong, and most powerfully peaceful, guiding his life and that of his wild companions by a book that he had consulted for years and in which he always found the help he needed—his Bible.

As the sun rose higher, the men, who had been paddling all the morning, needed rest. They landed and ate up the remnants of last night's supper with some biscuits spread with honey taken from the hollow of a tree where the wild bees had their hive. At noon, when the heat of the sun was beating down from a blue sky on the perspiring men, they started again.

Tired and sleepy, they landed at last, boiled the iguana that had been speared, and ate it for supper.

The men swiftly cut down branches and made little sheds by planting forked poles leaning toward one another with one at the top as the "roof tree." Then the branches were laid over the forked poles and tied to the roof tree with strips of bark while long grass as tall as a man was laid on like thatch to keep out the rain. The sheds were arranged round the campfire in a horseshoe, with room for the oxen in the middle. Each shed was closed at the back but open toward the campfire.

70

In an hour the men were under cover. In the clear white moonlight Livingstone came round to look at the sleeping forms of his companions and see that all were safe. He, too, after writing up his journal and asking his Father to protect the camp, crept into his gypsy tent and slept.

Then Mashauana, Livingstone's faithful head boatman, made his bed at the door of Livingstone's tent and lay down. The man or beast who harmed Livingstone on that journey would have had to do it over the body of Mashauana.

They traveled up the Zambezi till its banks turned east. Then they left it and struck westward on to the Kasai River, then northwest across the Kwango River to the Lucalla River, a tributary of the Coanza, and so— due west—to Loanda on the coast.

The journey in the land that Sekeletu governed was not very difficult. But as they got farther on they found that the wonderful conquests of Sekeletu's father had made the tribes beyond suspicious of them all. As they got nearer and nearer to the west coast, they found that the Portuguese slave trade had turned the Africans into grasping wretches, who not only refused food to Livingstone but would not let him pass through their country without gifts.

"Man, ox, gun, or tusk, you must give me," each chief would say. Then he would threaten that if the gift was

71

not at once forthcoming, Livingstone must go back—
or die.

"Man," of course, Livingstone absolutely refused to
give, for that meant selling a faithful friend into slavery;
"ox" he could rarely give, for he had few and those were
needed; "gun" he could not spare, for how then could
he get food for his followers; "tusk" he had, but only
a few. These tusks were from Sekeletu to make the
beginning of trade between the Makololo of Linyanti
and the Portuguese of Loanda.

One adventure of this kind happened among the
Chibokwe people. They reached the village of Njambi
on Saturday, March 4, 1854—just before Livingstone's
forty-first birthday. Wishing to have a restful Sunday,
they killed one of their riding oxen for food and sent
some of the meat as a present to Njambi, the chief. On
Sunday morning a messenger came with an ultimatum
from the chief.

"The chief," said the messenger impudently, "must
have a man, an ox, a gun, powder, some cloth, or a shell.
If not, you must go back."

Livingstone refused. In the afternoon his men were
thrown into great excitement by all the people of
Njambi coming and surrounding their encampment, the
younger warriors drawing their swords and brandishing
them in the face of the traveler with furious shouts.
Some pointed their guns at Livingstone, nodding to one

another as much as to say, "That is the way we shall do with him."

Livingstone sat calmly on his camp stool with his double-barreled hunting gun across his knees.

"Be seated," he said quietly to the chief, who—probably to his own surprise—found himself obeying.

"Why do you ask me to pay to walk on the ground of God, our common Father?" said Livingstone.

The chief could not answer this, for it was the custom of the African tribes to call the ground—except the gardens—common. But they still pressed him for a payment, most of all for a man to be given up as a slave. Livingstone would rather have died than do this. He offered a shirt; they asked for more. He added beads and a large handkerchief, but the more he offered the more they demanded. The armed young men rushed around brandishing weapons and shouting death.

It was a perilous moment. A young man rushed at Livingstone to kill him. Livingstone quickly put the muzzle of his gun to the young man's mouth—and the terrified youth ran for his life. Livingstone said, "We will not strike the first blow. If you do so, the guilt of blood is on your head."

His Makololo followers, armed with their hunting javelins, quickly surrounded the Chibokwe chief, Njambi. He, seeing that if his own men fired at Livingstone he himself would at once be killed by the Makololo, decided on peace. Presents were exchanged, and Livingstone and his party went on. The real blame for all this hateful greed lay, not on the Africans, but on the slave traders who had accustomed them to expect the present of a slave from every party that passed through the land.

One day Livingstone offered a tribe an ox, since they asked for one in payment for traveling through their land.

"No," they said, "we will not have it. Its tail has been cut and witchcraft medicine put in."

This gave Livingstone a good idea, at which his followers roared with laughter, for he cut the tuft off the end of the tail of each of the other oxen—and they never had another request for an ox.

He often used his projector at night and preached about the pictures. One chief, named Shinte, was especially eager to see the pictures. He gathered together all his people, including his many wives, for the grand sight. Livingstone showed first a picture of Abraham, with uplifted knife, about to sacrifice his son Isaac. The women listened silently while he explained it. But when he moved the slide to put in another, the picture of Abraham with his uplifted dagger seemed to move toward them.

"Mother, mother!" they all shouted at once and fled helter-skelter, tumbling over one another and knocking down the fetish huts in the dark. These are huts in which stand carved wooden figures, called fetishes, which the people believe to be inhabited by a spirit that must be fed to keep it good tempered.

Many of these people could not believe that Livingstone was a man. They thought that he was of a people who lived under the sea.

"Is that hair?" they would say as he took off his hat. "No. It is the mane of a lion and not hair at all."

"Mine," Livingstone replied, "is the real original hair; like yours was before it became scorched and frizzled in the sun!"

Then he would open his shirt and show his white chest, comparing it with his face, which the sun had burned a dark brown, almost as dark as theirs. They agreed that, as they always went about nearly naked in the sun, they had been scorched a brown-black and that they and Livingstone might really be brothers after all.

Livingstone's bad-tempered, broad-backed riding ox, Sinbad, came into use on this journey, when they all left the Zambezi and the canoes. Livingstone rode him, although he was so vicious, because his back was softer than the other oxen's, while his long horns were bent down and hung loosely, so that he could not hit his rider in the belt with them. Sinbad, however, would suddenly run off the track, and once ran just under a climber, which caught Livingstone and threw him off so that he struck his head.

While fording a stream one day, Sinbad stumbled in a hole in the bed of the river and flung Livingstone over his head into the water. One afternoon they came to a flooded stream called "Child of Loki," into which Sinbad dashed, sank, and threatened to turn over on Livingstone, who slipped off and struck out for the opposite bank. Thoroughly alarmed at this, twenty of his men rushed to his rescue—some in their eagerness leaping right in and letting their blankets float away down the stream. He reached the bank unaided, but there one seized his arm while another threw his arm round his body, anxious to help him out.

They were surprised to find that he could swim—though he swam like a frog while they swam like dogs. But it made him very happy to see that they cared for him so much. That night, when Livingstone was turning himself round and round in front of the fire to dry his clothes, the men who belonged to the village to which they had come tried to frighten Livingstone's African friends by telling them of the rivers that lay ahead.

They rolled with laughter, their eyes and white teeth flashing in the firelight as they pointed to Livingstone and said proudly:

"We can all swim; who carried the white man across the river but himself?"

76

These streams were swollen, and the valleys flooded because of the ceaseless rainfall during the latter part of the journey. The rain poured down, dripping from the trees in the forest and soaked through their sleeping blankets and skin rugs, as well as Livingstone's clothes, which now became moldy. The rain also was bad for the guns, causing them to rust, and it rotted the gypsy tent.

Often the only place where he could keep his watch dry was under his armpit, for he would be up to his waist in flood and marsh while the rain came down from above. Fever made Livingstone so weak that he could neither sit on the ox nor walk without support. Sometimes he just staggered on like one in a dream. But the White Man Who Would Go On refused to stop or turn back from his quest.

"Your white leader is only taking you to the coast to sell you as slaves," whispered some of the African villagers in the ears of his followers. What were they to believe? And they began to doubt and despair and threaten to turn back and go home.

"If you go back," said he to them, "still I shall go on."

Sick at heart and disappointed, he went into his little tent, feeling that he was alone—with his Father.

Looking up, he saw the head of one of his followers peering in at the little tent opening. It was Mohorisi, and the words he said were, "We will never leave you."

The others followed.

"We are all your children," they said. "We will die for you. We spoke in bitterness of spirit. You will see what we can do!"

Livingstone was glad again. And at last, after traveling for more than six months by canoe, on ox back, and on foot, through marsh and forest, through river and flood, in fever and hunger, in peril of savage men and wild beasts, over fifteen hundred miles of territory that no white man had ever seen before, Livingstone came out on a high plain in sight of the sea and the Portuguese city of Loanda—the goal of his journey.

His companions, who had never before seen the sea— or really believed in its existence—looked with wonder on the limitless blue ocean, sparkling in the sun.

"We marched along with our father," they said, "believing that what the ancients had always told us was true, that the world has no end; but all at once the world said to us, 'I am finished; there is no more of me!'"

8 : "The Forest Perilous"

During this great pathfinding journey from the interior to the west coast, Livingstone suffered terribly again and again from an awful fever that makes a man's head and all his body ache unbearably and weakens him till he cannot stand without help. Now that he had reached Loanda he greatly needed rest and medicine and was glad to stop for a while in a civilized town.

The Makololo were much interested in this strange new place. They looked at the Loanda houses in astonishment. Livingstone had on the journey tried to explain what a house two or three stories high was like, but they said that there could be no such thing as a hut on a hut, for the stakes of the top hut would have nothing to stick into. Besides, the roof of the hut was sloping—how could you put another on top of it? When they looked at a house for the first time, they said, "Ah! it is not a hut; it is a mountain with caves in it."

As they looked out to sea, they saw the gleaming sails of a ship that was steering toward the port. She was a British cruiser. When she came into port, the Makololo men were persuaded to go on board. They were amazed.

"It is not a canoe," they said. "It is a town! And what sort of town is it that you must climb into with a rope?"

The sailors on board were friendly with the Africans and gave them some of the bread and beef that they were having for dinner. The Africans got employment in unloading a coal boat. They could not understand how it held so much.

"We worked," they said, "from the rising till the setting sun for a moon and a half [six weeks] taking out stones that burn. We were tired, but there was still plenty left in the ship."

The captain of the British ship was very kind to Livingstone. "You are ill," he said when he landed and saw Livingstone's worn limbs and fever-stricken body. "You have worked and traveled without rest for fourteen years; all Britain will cheer to see you. Come home with us and rest—and see your wife and daughter and your sons again."

Ill, tired, and lonely, the invitation tempted him, but not for one second did he hesitate.

He looked at his Makololo companions who had risked life again and again and lived with him through all the perils of the pathfinding journey. He had brought them fifteen hundred miles from their homes. They called him their "father." They could not return alone. He turned his back to the sea and Britain, true to his word to a group of poor and friendly Africans.

Livingstone sent his journal home by ship, and the men started off on their tramp back to Linyanti. Many presents were given by the people of Loanda. There were a horse and brilliant colonel's uniform for Sekeletu, and two donkeys—for they, unlike the horses and oxen, are not killed by the tsetse fly.

The men were very proud of new costumes of striped cloth and red caps, which Mr. Gabriel, the British commissioner for suppressing the slave traffic and the only Englishman then living in Loanda, had given them. Livingstone was also glad to have a good new tent presented to him by the officers of the British cruiser. Orders were sent along the route by the Portuguese commandant that men must help and not hinder the travelers.

Some days after they had started back, they came

to some wonderful rocks that stood up like gigantic cliffs, three hundred feet high. The place was called Pungo Andongo. Here Livingstone got the news that the ship in which his journals were placed had been wrecked in a storm and had gone to the bottom of the sea. Eager as he was to go on, Livingstone settled there for three months and steadily rewrote all those hundreds of pages. It took from October till Christmas, but he knew that the very future of all that country would be affected by the knowledge of the land that he alone among all white men in the world had now obtained.

As Livingstone rode on Sinbad, the ox, from the heights of Pungo Andongo down among the date palms of the valley of Kassange, he came to the house of Captain Neves, a Portuguese, who lived at Kassange itself. While staying with him, Livingstone found a child sick with fever, whom he wished to make well. But the African mother believed that her boy was bewitched and would not listen to Dr. Livingstone when he wished to give the child the proper food and medicine. As a result, the child died.

An African man who was also ill in Kassange village said that his wife's sister had bewitched him. The witch doctor was going to put her through the ordeal of drinking poison to test her innocence, but Captain Neves stopped them, because the poison was very strong and would certainly have killed her. If she had died after submitting to the ordeal, they would have said, "That is a proof that she was a witch."

Livingstone found that in other parts of that valley of Kassange, where Captain Neves could not stop them, hundreds of people were killed year after year through this ordeal of poison. The witch doctors, whenever anyone was ill, would put on feathers and horns and dance and call out, as they smelled out the sorcerer who, they said, had bewitched the sick one. Then they would make the one accused of sorcery drink the poison and more often than not he would die. Livingstone saw that between the sorcerers and their enemies as many people were killed in a year as the slave trade destroyed. The people were filled with dread of the demon spirits of the dead, who would, they thought, do them harm. In spite of all the precautions taken by governments, many persons still die in Africa through such beliefs in sorcery and by poison. Not only do victims die by these poison ordeals, but, in many instances, they die from sheer terror of the curse cast on them by the evil spells of the sorcerer. In either event, death is evidence of the victim's guilt.

Livingstone thought what a tragedy it was that such evil acts should be done in such a fine country, just because the people believed in witches and demons instead of a Father God. Wherever the African tribes become Christian, the sorcerers and the witch doctors disappear because the African is certain that the power of Jesus Christ can overcome all demons as it did repeatedly in the gospel story.

Livingstone was thinking of these things one day in Kassange when, looking up, he saw running toward the house a man from Loanda with letters and papers. They were papers all the way from England addressed to himself. He eagerly opened them and read in the *Times* of London about the Crimean War, which was then being waged. There was the story of the dashing charge of the Light Brigade. To read this made him as excited as it does all people who admire daring. Livingstone himself did not carry lance and sword like a soldier; he was mounted, not on a dashing horse, but on a lumbering ox. In the very days, however, when he was reading in the *Times* of the brave soldiers, he was himself, like the Light Brigade, charging "into the valley of death," the valley of Kassange, to rescue the people there and in all Africa from the dread of the slave gang and witch doctors and demons.

He pushed on eastward back toward Linyanti, which was "home" for his companions.

One day the headman of a village came into Livingstone's camp and began quarreling. One of Livingstone's men lost his temper and gave him a blow on the mouth. This was the only time that one of Livingstone's men lost his temper on the whole journey, and this man was

84

the least brave of the whole company. They gave the headman a gun and five pieces of cloth to make up for the blow, but he asked for more. Livingstone refused the request.

So they departed, but suddenly, as Livingstone on his ox, followed by his men, wound along the path through the forest, they heard the crackling of branches and the sound of men rushing after them. The village men rushed out, hurled javelins, fired shots, and knocked burdens off the heads of some of Livingstone's carriers, hoping to make them flee and so to run off themselves with the plunder.

Livingstone was very ill with fever, but he forgot his sickness in this moment of danger, turned, staggered down the path toward the enemy, drew his revolver, with which he never shot a man, and threatened the chief with it. Livingstone's fearless face and the sight of the pistol aimed at him made the chief shake with fright.

"Oh! I have only come to speak to you. I wish peace only," he quavered.

They examined the chief's gun and found that he had just fired at them!

"We, too, wish peace," said Livingstone. "If you do, also, then go home to your village."

"I am afraid that you will shoot me in the back," answered the chief.

"If you are afraid of me, I am not afraid of you," replied Livingstone and calmly turned his back on the chief and mounted his ox.

Livingstone's men were so delighted with the result that they kept shouting to one another, saying what wonderful deeds they would have done if Livingstone had not stopped the fight.

Soon after this they met a man leading eight good-looking African women in a chain taking them to be sold for ivory tusks. A poor little slave girl, who was ill and too tall and slender for her age, turned aside from the slave party and was lost in the forest. Livingstone and his companions looked for her for a whole day, but they could not find her. She must have slept in the forest and, wakening, have wandered on and on until she dropped from exhaustion.

"*Ga ba na pelu* (They have no heart)," said Livingstone's Makololo men angrily of the slave traders.

They passed on, crossing rivers that ran northward into the Congo and walking through vast forests full of climbing plants so tough that one man had to go in front with a hatchet to clear the way. The narrow path zigzagged through the forest around the trunks of great trees that towered above them, making a green darkness as though they were walking at the bottom of a deep sea. There were no large animals in this forest—no antelopes feeding beside dark buffaloes but only mice and snakes. Livingstone longed to get back to the banks of the Zambezi where the animals abounded.

When they came to within ten miles of the bank of the Kasai River—a large tributary of the Congo—the chief, Kawawa, demanded an ox, gunpowder, a gun, and a robe—or a man as a slave—as payment for crossing.

"I shall stop you from crossing the river if you refuse," said Kawawa.

"I refuse," said Livingstone, who would not be bullied.

Then the African subjects of Kawawa rushed away for their bows, arrows, and spears with which to kill Livingstone and his men. Livingstone's men wanted to fight, but he told them to take up their luggage and march. They obeyed, and all the party moved off into the forest, the people of Kawawa gazing after them but not shooting.

When they reached the Kasai River, they found that four of Kawawa's men had rushed on and given orders to the ferryman to refuse a passage. The ferry canoe was taken away; the river was a hundred yards broad and was deep.

Livingstone thought of swimming over when the Kawawa people were gone. But after it was dark, Pitsane, one of Livingstone's men, went along the bank, found where the canoe was hidden, brought it along, ferried the party over, returned the canoe to its hiding place with some beads in it for good will, and swam back to Livingstone. They all went into camp and slept —though the Africans could not go to sleep for some time because they kept roaring with laughter at the faces the Kawawa would make the next morning when they found what had happened.

"Ah! ye are bad!" came a shout from the opposite side of the river in the morning from some of the Kawawa people as they saw Livingstone's party starting off.

"Ah! ye are good!" shouted Pitsane and the others. "We thank you for the loan of the canoe!"

They were rejoiced after many miles of dark forests to come out in sight of the waters of Lake Dilolo, with waves lashing its shore. Having said good-by to the Lord of Dilolo, a fat, jolly chief, they passed on and were glad once more to be among the friendly tribes of the Zambezi.

All the women of Libonta, the first village of Sekeletu to which they came, rushed out with joyous shouts of welcome, dancing and waving sticks as the party approached. The diviners of the tribe had long ago said that Livingstone and all his men were dead; yet here they were back again, and—in spite of all perils and fever—every one of the twenty-eight was alive.

The Libonta people gave oxen, milk, meal, and butter to Livingstone and his men. Strangers flocked in from a distance. Livingstone held a thanksgiving service, at which his men dressed themselves up in their beautiful new suits with red caps, which were given to them at Loanda. They tried to walk stiffly like the soldiers they had seen at Loanda, called themselves Livingstone's *batlabain* or "braves," and enjoyed being the center of admiration of all the women and children.

At last they reached Linyanti, the home of the Makololo, in triumph. Livingstone was amused at the pride of his men as they strutted into the village with their new clothes, which they had carefully carried all the way from Loanda. He heard them boasting, "We went on till we had finished the whole world. We only turned when there was no more land!"

9 : "Sounding Smoke"

The Pathfinder had now discovered a way from the heart of Africa out to the Atlantic. He had brought back his men. But it was a hard and fever-stricken path. He wondered if there might not be a better way down the Zambezi to the east coast.

Chief Sekeletu was proud of having helped Livingstone. He now loved him more than ever. So Sekeletu gave Livingstone one hundred and twenty of his men to go with him down the Zambezi and thirteen oxen for riding and for food.

Once more they started out on "the long trail," this

time going east instead of west. They came quickly to a patch of forest where the tsetse fly—so deadly to horses and oxen—lived. Men went on in advance to make a camp while Livingstone with some younger men waited to take the animals through at night when the tsetse fly sleeps.

They started at night through the trees in pitch darkness when flash after flash of a thunderstorm burst upon them. The lightning spread in eight or ten forks across the sky while sheet lightning, which made the whole country visible, was followed by dense darkness and deafening thunderclaps that made the horses tremble. The young men were not afraid but laughed as they bumped against one another in the darkness.

The rain came rushing down, and the night was cold after the heat of the day. All their bedding and the tent had gone on, yet they could never get through the storm to where the camp had settled. So they turned aside to a campfire that had been deserted by whoever had lighted it. Livingstone lay down in his wet clothes on the cold ground to try to sleep. He felt a touch and looking up saw Sekeletu.

"Here, my father, is my blanket," said the young chief. "You take it to keep you warm."

Sekeletu would not be refused. He wrapped the blanket round Livingstone and went off to lie down uncovered on the cold, damp ground.

They went on down the Chobe to the great Zambezi. Some paddled along the river in canoes while others drove the oxen on the banks. One day Livingstone saw five strange columns of vapor rising in the air miles ahead, and he heard the sound of distant booming in the air.

"It is *Mosi-oa-tunya* (Sounding Smoke)," said the Makololo.

The river rolled on more and more swiftly. Slowly and carefully the Africans guided the canoe out of the rushing waters into the quieter eddies in the center of the stream behind an island. Livingstone landed, crept to the very edge of the island, and looked over. A breathtaking sight met his eyes. The mighty river, more than a mile wide at this point, rolled over the edge of a precipice, dashing down four hundred feet with the mighty roar of many waters.

It fell sheer into a narrow zigzag chasm, where it went seething and rushing between gigantic cliffs of rock. The spray rose in five great columns that hid the sun. In the spray hung a many-colored double rainbow, a beautiful bridge of quietness over the rage of the tumbling water.

It was November, 1855. Livingstone was the first white man who ever saw "Sounding Smoke," the falls that are much larger than Niagara Falls. He named them the Victoria Falls after the Queen of England. On the island at the brink of the falls, he carved his initials on the trunk of a tree.

He left the Zambezi, with its dark Africans who were almost black, and marched northeast to the higher ground, where the people were a light coffee color. He found this higher land more healthful and hoped that it might be—as it is—a place where missionaries could work.

From this country of gentle hills, the party began to march down the gradual slope that was to lead them to the east coast. They had now come into new dangers, for they were at the end of their own Makololo country and had come to the land where the Batlea lived. These men were rebels against Sekeletu's rule.

Some of these savage men came up in the evening and tried to spear a young Makololo who had gone for water. One of them rushed at Livingstone with glaring eyes and foaming lips howling hideously and swinging a battle-ax. Livingstone showed no fear but looked the man steadily in the face. His own men obeyed his orders not to knock the frenzied savage on the head. But Sekwebu, a Makololo, held his spear ready to kill the man if he really struck at Livingstone. Livingstone simply asked one of the Batlea who was more friendly to take this madman away. He was obeyed.

On the next day Livingstone went up onto the rocks

with his instruments to work out the right direction for their journey. Looking through his glass, he saw two miles off an elephant and her calf. The calf was rolling in the mud; its mother fanned herself with her great ears.

A line of Livingstone's men were closing round the animals, who were quietly enjoying themselves, unsuspicious of danger. With spears in hand the men approached, and the elephants became aware of the danger. The calf ran forward, but the men turned it back shouting and singing, "O chief! Chief! We have come to kill you."

The mother elephant placed herself between the men and her calf and fled across the rivulet. The men came closer and hurled their javelins at her. Livingstone had sent orders that they were not to kill the calf, but before Sekwebu, the messenger, reached the rivulet the men had speared it. The elephant charged at them again and again, but they hid behind trees each time. At last, wounded by many javelins, she sank slowly to her knees and died.

A perilous adventure met Livingstone when he came to the place where the Loangwa River runs into the Zambezi on its north bank. Men, half Portuguese, half African, had some time before angered the chief, who now thought that Livingstone was of the same race. He threatened Livingstone, who opened his shirt, showed the chief his white skin where it had not been tanned by the sun.

"Are the Bazinka like that?" he asked.

"No," said the chief, "they are not."

Livingstone could see, however, that it was more than likely that the still suspicious chief would give orders for him to be knocked on the head and killed on the following day when he was to cross the river.

Should he cross secretly by night, he asked himself, and so escape?

He felt no fear for himself, thinking only that it would be a pity for all the discoveries that he had made for the opening up of this country to be utterly lost. He opened his tin box, took from it his Bible, and in the flickering light read:

"Go ye therefore and teach all nations, . . . and lo, I am with you always."

"It is," he told himself, "the word of a Gentleman of the most sacred and strictest honor. I will not cross furtively by night as I intended. It would appear as flight, and should such a man as I flee? Nay, verily, I shall take observations for latitude and longitude to-night, though they may be the last."

In the morning the threatening natives came, all armed with spears, and gathered around Livingstone and his men as they went to the banks of the river to cross in the one canoe that was lent to them. It looked as though the natives would let some of the party go across and then slay the others.

First the Makololo carried their burdens over in the big canoe, then the oxen. The men followed. Livingstone stayed till the last. But while the canoe was going to and fro he took out his watch, his magnifying lens, and other things from his pocket. He showed these armed and threatening savage Africans how to burn with the lens by focusing the sun's rays through it. He let them listen to the ticking of his watch while he explained how it told the time. They came close round him listening, looking, and asking questions.

When his companions had crossed, Livingstone thanked the armed natives for lending the canoe to him.

"I wish you peace," said Livingstone and, entering the canoe, was paddled across the river. No man raised a spear to harm him.

Most of the people in the villages on this journey had been kind to them and given them food. Since there were more than a hundred in Livingstone's party, this meant that the people had been very generous.

"Did I not tell you," said Sekwebu, Livingstone's headman, "that these people have hearts?"

"Yes," answered some of his companions. "Look! Although we have been so long away from home, not one of us has become lean."

As they got nearer and nearer to the Portuguese on

the east coast, however, they found the dark trail of the slave trade. The minds of the people there were poisoned against them because they had seen men with smooth hair and brown faces—like Livingstone—carry off their children into slavery.

Livingstone wished to cross to the south bank of the Zambezi because of a war that had been going on between the Portuguese and the Africans on the north bank. He came toward the village of Mpende, who sent him no messengers—a sign that he was an enemy. At sunrise a party of Mpende's people, waving red rags and shouting with hideous screams, came toward Livingstone's camp and lighted a fire, into which they threw magic charms. They believed that these charms would harm Livingstone's party. They then turned and disappeared.

Armed men were now moving from all quarters toward Livingstone's camp. His own men were in fighting fettle and desired nothing more than to put their javelins into Mpende.

"You have seen us with elephants," said some of the hotheaded young men to Livingstone as they shook their spears in the direction of the village, "but you don't know yet what we can do with men."

Livingstone, as he always did, sternly forbade them to strike at all, except in defense of themselves. Mpende sent spies to watch them. To two of these spies Livingstone gave the leg of an ox and said, "Take this to Mpende. I wish peace."

Soon after this two gray-haired, wrinkled men came from Mpende and looking out with curious eyes at Livingstone asked, "Who are you?"

"I am a Lekoa [an Englishman]," he replied.

"We do not know that tribe," they said. "We suppose that you are a Mozunga [a Portuguese], the tribe with which we have been fighting."

Livingstone showed them the white skin of his chest and asked, "Have they skin like that?"

"No," said the old men of Mpende's village. "We never saw skin so white as that." Then after a pause they added, "Ah! You must be one of that tribe that has heart to [loves] the black men."

"Yes, indeed," said Livingstone, "that is my tribe." He was glad to think that even in the middle of Africa the people had heard that white men of the Anglo-Saxon race "had heart to" them.

Sekwebu, Livingstone's headman, went to talk to Mpende, who, when he had made up his mind not to fight him but to be friendly, said, "Well, the white man ought to cross to the other side of the river. This bank is hilly and rough, and the way to Tette is shorter on the other side."

"But who will take us across?" asked Sekwebu.

"You shall cross," said Mpende, by which he meant

98

that he was now real "friends" with them and would lend the canoes.

They all crossed to the south bank of the Zambezi in large canoes, leaving the whole of Mpende's tribe, which had been so threatening when they came, full of friendliness and good will.

His own men made Livingstone their hero more and more after this. They saw what power he had to win men to his way, and they heard—both from free men and from slaves whom they met—that the white men of Livingstone's tribe were as brothers and not as slave drivers among the Africans.

One day, going along the bank of the Zambezi, they met some African traders carrying bundles of calico. Livingstone produced two small elephant tusks and offered them to the traders in return for some clothing for his men, many of whom were now naked. He found that the calico had come all the way from America, for it was stamped "Lawrence Mills, Lowell."

Soon after this the men chased and slew an elephant for food. There was too much for them to eat then, and it would not stay fresh in the heat. Hyenas gathered round the camp and kept up a loud laughter for two whole nights.

"What are the hyenas laughing at?" asked Livingstone of his men.

"They are laughing," the Makololo replied, "because

we cannot eat it all and shall have to leave plenty for them!"

As they went on, Livingstone enjoyed watching all the animals that roamed over the country from the elephant and the fierce black rhinoceros to the tiniest insects all happy at their work. For instance, when he was waiting by the side of this dead elephant, he saw insects like grains of sand running about on his tin box. He took his magnifying glass and saw one insect all green and gold tidying its tiny wings, another as clear as a piece of crystal, a third a brilliant red, while another was jet-black. Everywhere he found something to wonder about.

In the forest he listened to the hum of the insects flying and the singing of the birds. Their voices were, he said, like English birds singing in a foreign language. Some were like the lark, two like the thrush; others brought the chaffinch, the robin, and the startled blackbird to his mind. One bird would sound a note like the twanging of a violin string, another said slowly, "Peek, pak, pok." The turtledoves murmured, "Pumpura, pumpura," while the honey guide—which would lead Livingstone to the hives of the wild bees—said, "Chicken, chik, churr, churr." Near the villages the cheeky mockingbird would make them laugh by imitating the roosters and hens.

On March 2, 1856, Livingstone, who was worn with

22882

travel and lack of food, could go no farther. He lay down to rest about eight miles from Tette on the Zambezi, where a Portuguese commandant lived. He sent messages on to the commandant. About two o'clock in the morning the Makololo were frightened by the sudden appearance of a company of soldiers with two officers.

"We are captured!" they cried as they woke Livingstone.

But the soldiers had come bringing a fine breakfast, which Livingstone said was the most refreshing that he had ever eaten in his life! He eagerly walked the last eight rough miles to Tette. After resting there, he went on in a large canoe to Quilimane, the port from which he was to sail to Britain, which he had not seen for sixteen years. Nor had he spoken a word of English for three and a half years.

The time came for him to sail and leave his Makololo men. He settled most of them at Tette on plantations. Some went with him to Quilimane. They said that they would go on with him to Britain and find Ma-Robert and her children.

Livingstone told them that they must wait in Africa for his return. He could not pay for their passage on the steamer to England.

"Nothing but death will prevent my return," he assured them.

101

"Nay, Father," they replied, "you will not die. You will return to take us back to Sekeletu."

One man stayed with him to the end, pleading with Livingstone to take him on board ship.

"You will die," said Livingstone, "if you go to such a cold country as mine."

"That is nothing," said the African. "Let me die at your feet."

PART IV

10 : *Facing Poisoned Arrows*

Livingstone reached home in time to have a merry Christmas with his three boys and Agnes in 1856. He had such games with them as they had never had in their lives, for when they were quite small in Africa he seemed to have no time for playing with his children. When the spring came, the British flowers and birds made him quite excited. He had not seen them for so long.

"We have," he said joyfully, "seen daisies, primroses, hawthorns, and robin redbreasts."

Lions and elephants seemed quite dull compared

with robins! He used to take the children for walks in the summer in the Barnet woods near London and would suddenly run off, plunge in among the ferns and shrubs, and hide while they would search for him. Then he would startle them by coming out just where they did not expect him.

Ma-Robert hardly knew what to do for joy at seeing him after so many years. She wrote a little poem to her husband when he was on his way home, and when he at last came to her, he read it. This is one stanza:

A hundred thousand welcomes! how my heart is gushing
   o'er
With the love and joy and wonder thus to see your face
   once more.
How did I live without you these long, long years of woe?
It seems as if 'twould kill me to be parted from you now.

He went to see his own mother. His father, who had seen him off from the quay at Glasgow sixteen years earlier, had died just before Livingstone reached home. The traveler, who had faced lions and the spears of savages without a tremor of weakness, broke down and burst into tears when he saw his father's empty chair. He had so looked forward to talking over his adventures with his father.

Ma-Robert and the children could not have him all to themselves, even at home in Britain, for he was now one of the most famous men in all the land. He was obliged to go to scientific societies, to meetings, and to universities, to make speeches—which he disliked very much—and to receive medals of honor. They also made him write a book about his adventure. It is called *Missionary Travels.*

One day he went to see the boys and girls of Queen Victoria, the eldest of whom afterwards became King Edward VII. They enjoyed hearing about the adventures of this strong, brown-faced traveler. On another day he went to see Queen Victoria herself. She laughed very much when, after telling her how glad he was that now he could tell the Africans that he had really seen his chief, he said, "The first question they will ask will be, 'How many cows has she got?'"

The Africans, having no money, he explained, reckoned their wealth chiefly by cattle, though some also by tusks.

One day he went to Glasgow to be made a Doctor of Laws, because of his great discoveries. The undergraduates came, as was usual in those days, armed with peashooters, trumpets, and noisy rattles all ready to stamp and shout and make fun in the gallery.

Livingstone walked in with his strong, resolute "forward-tread," his face burned brown by the African sun and seamed with the lines of pain through many fevers. His left arm hung limp. The students remembered the lion bite and all the thousand perils this plain, sunburned man had faced. The rattles and the trumpets were silent; no peashooter was used, not a foot stamped. They listened in perfect silence to this man whom they felt to be the greatest hero they had seen.

He told them about some of his perils and adventures. Then he asked, "Shall I tell you what sustained me amidst the toil, the hardship, and loneliness of my exiled life? It was the promise, 'Lo, I am with you always, even unto the end.'"

He was happiest when he was enjoying himself among friends rather than when speaking at big meetings. He liked boys especially. One day he went to see a boy who was ill. He told the boy his lion adventure story and then he took off his coat, turned up his shirt sleeve, and showed the boy the very tooth marks that the lion had made in his arm.

A boy in his first week in geography class today can learn more about African lakes, rivers, and mountains than the wisest men knew before Livingstone came back to Britain. They had said, "Africa is a great desert." Livingstone showed them for the first time that it is full of great rivers and lakes. They had said, "The Africans are all cruel, fighting savages." Livingstone showed them that, when treated kindly, the Africans were faithful friends, like his Makololo.

Livingstone, however, wanted to find out still more.

He wished to discover some high, healthful place in Central Africa where white men could train African teachers and preachers. He planned to open up paths through the jungles and explore the rivers so thoroughly that they should become the highways of the nations. He believed that the coming of white settlers and European trade to Central Africa would hinder the slavers in their cruel business. To strike the deathblow of the slave trade was growing to be a great purpose of his life.

To be quite free to go anywhere as he thought best, he gave up his position under the London Missionary Society. The government gave him the powers of a British consul. In the early spring of 1858, a government ship, the *Pearl*, steamed out from the quay at Liverpool with Livingstone, Ma-Robert, and their youngest boy Oswell waving handkerchiefs to the friends who had come to say good-by. When the *Pearl* reached Cape Town, they met Grandfather Moffat. Mrs. Livingstone stayed with her father and mother while Livingstone steamed up the east coast to where the many mouths of the Zambezi ran through mangrove swamps and jungle into the sea.

Strange steel plates, engines, and a funnel were hoisted out from the hold of the *Pearl*. When screwed together they made a little steam launch, which was christened the *Ma-Robert*, after Mrs. Livingstone. The

109

Pearl and the *Ma-Robert* then sailed up the Kongone, the deepest mouth of the Zambezi.

Great palms stood up like church spires on the banks. Bright yellow hibiscus flowers flamed along the bank. Wild date palms and huge ferns waved their fronds as the boats passed. Bright kingfishers shot along like streaks of light and then settled down again to watch from a tree stump. The dignified fish hawk sailed away on his great wings while the shining ibis rose and flew off shrieking, "Ha, ha, ha!"

Along the river the travelers saw, among the banana and coco palms, Africans scampering down the ladders in front of their native huts, which were built on legs above the marshy ground. These swamp dwellers opened their eyes, astonished at the puffing steamers.

"It is a village," said one old man as he stood on the deck of the *Pearl*. "Is it made out of one tree like our canoes?"

The natives paddled along behind the steamer in their swift canoes shouting, *"Malonda"* (things for sale), and holding up fowls and baskets of rice.

At last the *Pearl* and *Ma-Robert* steamed out of the Kongone into the main stream of the broad Zambezi. The river here was too shallow for the *Pearl*, so they put her stores on shore at Shupanga, a Portuguese settlement, and the *Ma-Robert* launch went on alone. She snorted and puffed, yet for all her fussy noise went very slowly. Her furnaces burned wood only, and it took three days to cut enough wood to drive her for two days. She was a great disappointment to Livingstone, who nicknamed her the "*Asthmatic*," because she was so wheezy.

At last, however, she paddled up to Tette, where Dr. Livingstone had left his Makololo friends. He went ashore, and at once they rushed down and shouted with joy at seeing him.

"They said that you would not come back," cried the Africans, "but we trusted you."

Some were so overjoyed that they ran to put their arms round him, but the others scolded them, and said, "Don't touch him, you will spoil his new clothes!"

The Makololo climbed aboard the "*Asthmatic*," and the party went on up the river. They came to a place where the Zambezi tumbled over rocks and swirled round boulders through miles of shallow rapids.

Here Livingstone, his friend Dr. Kirk—whom the British government sent to accompany him as a botanist and as a younger companion—and some Makololo left the launch. They waded along the shallow stream and scrambled over the boulders till, with much difficulty, they reached the other end of the rapids.

Right up in front of them stood a great mountain, at the foot of which the Zambezi flowed. Their guide

111

said, "The river is all smooth above here. I have hunted there. I know."

So they turned back, thinking these rapids exhausted all the difficulties of steaming up the river.

That night, as they sat in camp around their fire, two Africans came and said, "The guide has told you wrong. It is not all smooth water above. There is a cataract called Morumbwa." Livingstone turned to the guide, asking if this was so.

"I will not take you there," said the guide. "No man can reach it—nor could an elephant, a hippopotamus, or a crocodile."

Livingstone determined to go.

The mountains rose three thousand feet high on either side of the river like a huge trough, all black rock and thornbush. The men jumped from crag to boulder and crawled round the edges of a cliff where a false step would have hurled the whole party into boiling eddies of the river. The sun beat down on the black rock till it was so hot that they could not bear to put their hands on it. The bare feet of the Makololo were blistered. Livingstone heard their grumbling.

"We thought he had a heart. He has none. No one can walk here and live. He has gone mad."

At last they heard the roar of waters and came to the Morumbwa Cataract, where the mile-wide river, caught at a bend in the mountains, was jammed in a space fifty yards wide and poured down in one boiling flood.

The cataract was beautiful, but it meant a barrier against Livingstone's aim, for he wished to find a way for trade to go by water up into the heart of Africa. He found that the cataract could be passed by a powerful steamer when the river was in full flood, but the "*Asthmatic*" was useless for this, and the river was now low.

"Let us turn off from the Zambezi and travel up the unexplored tributary, the Shire," said Livingstone when they got back to Shupanga.

"It is impossible," replied the Portuguese and the Africans of that settlement, explaining that the river was choked with duckweed and that the natives would shoot them with poisoned arrows. Livingstone, however, spent his whole life doing things that men said were impossible. So they turned the bow of the steam launch up the Shire, on which no white man had ever traveled before. As they looked out at the banks, they saw natives with bows and arrows, dodging behind trees and taking aim at them.

Five hundred armed Africans gathered on the bank at a village over which Chief Tingane ruled. He had never allowed any Portuguese to go up, nor any Africans to come down, the river. He was a gray-haired man over six feet tall. The fierce savages all shouted for the

113

steamer to go back and threatened to kill the travelers with their poisoned arrows.

Taking his life in his hands, Livingstone, unarmed and unprotected, went ashore—alone among this horde of warlike, angry savages.

The very daring of his calm, smiling approach to a terrible death seemed to awe them.

"I am come," he said, "in peace. I will not make slaves. I am English. I wish to find a path so that we may come and buy cotton from you. There is one Father above all, whose children we all are, whether brown or white. He is displeased if we sell or buy our brothers."

Tingane thought this was good and made friends at once. The steamer was allowed to go on up the river. They went on for two hundred miles till they came to six foaming cataracts, which they called the Murchison Falls. They could go no farther by water with the *Ma-Robert*.

The *"Asthmatic"* now leaked in a thousand places so that the cabin was always wet and, therefore, full of mosquitoes. But she snorted her way back down the Shire and up the Zambezi to Tette and then again on a second voyage to these Shire cataracts.

Wonderful sights met Livingstone at every bend of the river. There were pineapple and orange and lemon trees. Monkeys swung from the creepers, hawks swooped down for fish, and antelopes fled among the trees.

In one great marsh he counted eight hundred elephants and captured a little one. He told his son Tom about this in a letter to England. It was, he said, "about the size of the largest dog you ever saw, but one of the Makololo, in a state of excitement, cut its trunk so that it bled very much and died in two days. Had it lived, we should have sent it to the Queen, as no African elephant was ever seen in England."

One day they shot two enormous pythons ten feet long.

From the masthead of the steamer Livingstone watched the long-necked cormorants take "headers" into the stream while big-pouched pelicans swam on the water and long-legged herons stared into the water for fish. Little weaver birds—all red and yellow—chattered to their mates in their hanging nests among the grass. Pretty little hawks darted after glittering dragonflies.

Landing, they marched—forty-two in all—northeast along the bank of a flowing stream. They then started to climb the Manganja Hills, looking back from the height to the silver stream, the green forests, and the distant blue mountains. The air was cool, and they slept under the trees since they were now above the damp river land where the mosquitoes live.

They found the beautiful Lake Shirwa. Later on their path they followed the Shire above the Murchison Cataracts, until at last, just before midday on September 16, 1859, the waters of Lake Nyasa gleamed before them, stretching away beyond the limits of sight. Livingstone was the first white man who ever saw Lake Nyasa. They slept that night at the foot of a giant banyan tree, where four could lie between two of the enormous serpent roots.

Dealers came to them there offering boys and girls for sale as slaves. When Livingstone said that they were Anglo-Saxons, the men were afraid. They decamped and ran off during the night, for they knew that the British were trying to stop this horrible wrong to Africa.

The Makololo grasped their spears. Their hands twitched, and their eyes gleamed with anger as they saw their brother Africans being carried off into slavery.

"Oh," they said to Livingstone, their voices hoarse with wrath, "why won't you let us choke them?"

11 : The Smoke of Burning Villages

Livingstone sat down and wrote long letters home to Britain, saying, "Come out and found a colony here: send missionaries, farmers, workers."

Newly captured slaves were being carried across Lake Nyasa packed in rakish Arab *dhows,* swift sailing ships used on the east coast of Africa and in the Indian Ocean. He saw that a single British steamer on that lake could stop its slave traffic. He looked on its lovely shores and the green hillsides and imagined those paths no longer threaded by wretched slave gangs but alive with a missionary colony of British and American people.

While waiting for an answer to his letters, he sailed back down the Shire and Zambezi to Tette in the snorting "*Asthmatic*," which now leaked at every joint while her engines clanked and groaned at every stroke.

He landed at Tette and then carried out his old promise and led his Makololo back to their own land, which they had left years before. They struggled back along the old trail, past the Victoria Falls to Linyanti.

It made him sad to see that all the missionaries who had gone to teach the Makololo had died and that his friend the young chief Sekeletu was ill.

He watched the Makololo girls and boys playing their games. One game was that of carrying a little girl on the shoulders of two others, who walked about with her, while all the others clapped their hands. The children stopped before each hut and sang pretty airs, beating time with stamping of feet and clapping of hands.

Most of their play was "Let's pretend." The girls "made believe" they were mothers, building little huts, making small pots, hoeing tiny gardens, cooking and pounding corn. The boys flung spears made of reed and pointed with wood and carried small shields or shot at trees with small bows and arrows, or they made little cattle pens into which they drove cows they had made of clay—even to the quaintly curved horns.

The people watched him. One Makololo woman—Tselane—seeing Dr. Livingstone making scientific observations with his instruments, laughed and said roguishly, "Poor thing, playing like a little child!"

He traveled back down to the Zambezi again, some of his Makololo friends still keeping with him. The old "*Asthmatic*," that mosquito-haunted, groaning, wheezing steamer, finally ran aground on a sand bank and sank to the bottom of the river.

In answer to Livingstone's letters, however, a new vessel was on its way out—the splendid little steamer *Pioneer*, which had only one drawback: she drew five feet of water instead of three, with the result that she was always running aground on sand banks.

A group of men waved their hands to Livingstone from the deck of the *Pioneer* as she steamed into the Zambezi. They were Bishop Mackenzie and a band of missionaries sent out by Oxford and Cambridge Universities in England to work in the Shire Valley. They steamed with him up to the Murchison Cataracts and then walked up to the highlands near Lake Nyasa.

In front of them a cruel gang of Portuguese had gone, saying, "We are the children of Dr. Livingstone."

The natives for love of Livingstone had welcomed them and then had found themselves in the grip of the slave trader.

Around the corner of a hill came a long line of men,

119

women, and children, chained and roped to one another, with slave sticks riveted around the necks of the men. African slave drivers, with muskets on their shoulders, swaggered along in triumph, beating the wretched captives and blowing with pride on long tin horns.

Their leader caught sight of Livingstone. His face changed. He gave the alarm. In a moment the jaunty bullies were flying like mad into the forest. The soles of their cowardly feet and their red caps were all that could be seen.

With joyful eagerness Livingstone and his friends drew their knives and cut the bonds of the women and children. Then he took a saw and cut through the slave sticks that were round the necks of the men. With the slave sticks they made a jolly bonfire to boil breakfast for all the starving company of freed slaves.

A little boy—a slave ten minutes before but now free—came up to Livingstone and his men and said, "The others tied and starved us, you cut the ropes and tell us to eat. What sort of people are you? Where did you come from?"

These freed slaves were the beginning of the bishop's mission church.

The smoke of burning villages, the shouts of triumphant warriors, and the wail of Manganja women met Livingstone two days later. Around the hillside came Ajawa warriors with their Manganja captives.

Taunting words to the Ajawa from some persons who were standing behind Livingstone angered the Ajawa, who began to shoot poisoned arrows. On they came, dancing hideously. Livingstone's party were obliged to fire their rifles to frighten the Ajawa away. It was the first time he had ever failed to make peace, and that was because of the people who had, from his side, shouted to the others.

Livingstone left the bishop to found his mission at Magomero on Lake Nyasa. Then he turned back and traveled down the Shire again. He was eager and excited. Ma-Robert—whom he had not seen since he left her at Cape Town—had given birth to a little daughter while staying with her mother at Kuruman, had gone home to Britain to see the other children, and was now coming out to join him again. As her ship steamed down the mouth of the Zambezi, she saw her husband standing on the paddle box of the *Pioneer* as it put out to meet her.

Only a few weeks later, at Shupanga on the Zambezi, the fever struck her down. Livingstone, with his new friend Dr. Stewart, who had brought her to him from Britain, nursed her with tenderest care. But slowly she sank. Her death filled the brave Pathfinder with a sadness that went with him ever after in all his travels.

With an aching heart he left the Zambezi. The weeks and months that followed were sad and discouraging for Livingstone. He longed to go home to comfort his motherless children. He often wished for rest.

But the Pathfinder could not rest till his work was done. He kept on bravely, trying to finish his explorations. He attempted to find a shorter way to Lake Nyasa by the Rovuma River. Failing in this, he turned back down to the sea, along the coast, and up the Zambezi and Shire again.

This time he tugged behind the *Pioneer* the little *Lady Nyasa*, a steamer built for Lake Nyasa. All up the valley were burned out villages, the skeletons of starved and slaughtered Africans, the hideous trail of the slave trade.

A letter from England from the government called Livingstone home, but he could not return at once for it was the dry season, and the *Pioneer* could not float down till some months later when the rainy season would fill the river.

While he was waiting, he started once more for Lake Nyasa with a boat borne by bearers past the cataracts. They had passed all the rapids save the last. The Makololo put the boat into smooth, swift-running water between these rapids and towed it up till they came near to the last rapid when they pulled it to the bank.

"We will show you how to manage a boat!" shouted some of the Zambezi men. They took the rope from the hands of the Makololo. Three of them jumped into the boat; two hauled at the rope. The rapids caught her bow, twisted her round, and snatched the rope from the hands of the Zambezi men.

She turned bottom upward and swung round in an eddy. Then away she went like an arrow down the cataracts.

The crestfallen Zambezi men came to shore, bowed at Livingstone's feet, and asked forgiveness. Annoyed as he was, he did not like "crying over spilt milk." He just sent them back to the *Pioneer* to carry up food, cloth, and beads to replace those lost in the boat and walked on.

He marched on with one white friend and a few Makololo companions round to the west of Lake Nyasa northward till he came within ten days' march of another lake, Bangweolo. He turned back before he reached it, for the rainy season was on them, and he would now be able to steam the *Pioneer* and *Lady Nyasa* down the Zambezi and so go home to Britain.

He thought that he might sell the useful *Lady Nyasa* to some seafaring trader at Zanzibar. A government cruiser—the *Ariel*—took in tow the "Lady of the Lake," as Livingstone loved to call his little steamer, and towed her up the coast to Mozambique.

Suddenly, out of the north, there swept a fearful hurricane that lashed the ocean to fury and drove the *Ariel* back in her tracks. She swept down on the *Nyasa*

123

stern foremost. The hawser, becoming entangled with the screw, stopped her engines.

It seemed that nothing could save Livingstone, for the great vessel loomed overhead and seemed about to crush the little steamer. But the *Ariel* just scraped past the bow of the *Lady Nyasa* without harming her.

In the rolling ocean it was hard and dangerous work to get another hawser from the man-of-war to Livingstone's steamer so that the *Ariel* could go on towing her up the coast. A cask was hurled into the sea from the *Ariel* with a hawser attached; then one of Livingstone's men, with another cable, jumped overboard into the boiling sea, tied the cable to the cask, and the *Ariel* hawser was thus drawn on board and secured. Then the *Ariel* drove ahead and towed the *Lady Nyasa* in the teeth of the storm to Mozambique.

When Livingstone had cleaned his steamer at Mozambique, he went on to Zanzibar. He made inquiries and found that he could not sell her there, for the only men who would buy wanted her for carrying slaves! Yet he had spent all the money that he had in building the "Lady of the Lake." What was he to do?

He would rather see her at the bottom of the Indian Ocean than in the slavers' hands. So he formed a plan— the most dangerous of all the adventures of his life.

For in that little vessel Livingstone, with a crew of men who had never been to sea and with only fourteen tons of coal on board, started to sail across the wide Indian Ocean. The men soon learned to climb along a boom, reeve a rope through the block at the end, take the end of the rope in their teeth, and climb back—each pitch of the boat dipping them into the sea.

Day after day Livingstone stood at the helm under the sweltering sun guiding his little vessel over the ocean by the knowledge that the captain of the *George* had given him, thirty years before, as a young man on his first voyage out.

The wind dropped. He had to save his coal for steaming down the coast of India to Bombay. They lay becalmed in the Indian Ocean, with sails flapping on the rolling mast and the blistering sunshine beating upon their heads, watching the cruel sharks, the sporting dolphins, and the flying-fish, as they chased and fled from one another in the still sea.

The sky changed, the wind moaned, the tempest broke. The little *Lady Nyasa* was tossed on the boundless sea with the gale whistling through her rigging, and her captain, still undaunted, clinging to the wheel and gazing out into the storm. The hissing breakers swept past with crests curling as though they would swallow her or dash her to the bottom of the ocean. But she swam from trough to crest of the waves, first her nose and then her stern in the air as she plowed through the seas.

125

The boat seemed alive with the dauntless spirit of her captain. She shook off the waves from her streaming deck and drove on through the storm, till at last she crept unnoticed into Bombay harbor.

Livingstone took ship home from India. Britain rose, with flags waving and surging cheers, to welcome the hero scout of Africa. Those who saw him then remembered him long afterwards as a smallish, sturdy man with the face of a warrior and eyes that looked right through them—keen and gentle. He lectured and spoke all over the land, stirring the country against the slave traffic; he wrote a book, *The Zambezi and Its Tributaries*, full of stories of those broken-hearted African children driven from their burning villages. The Heart of Britain itself burned to free Africa.

Then he took ship once more—for Africa. He stood in the stern to take his last look at the shores of England and the sad row of fluttering handkerchiefs that waved farewell.

He never saw Britain again.

PART V

12 : On the Slave Trail

The fierce African sun beat down upon the white walls of Zanzibar as it looked out from its island over the glittering sea to Africa. Livingstone walked along the evil smelling streets into an open square. The shouts of angry masters, the hum of bargaining, and the snarling of many dogs filled the air.

He saw herded there hundreds of Africans—naked boys with flashing teeth, young women who hung their heads with burning shame, fathers whose eyes shone with hate and loathing, mothers who wept because their children had been taken from them.

Among the Africans swaggered tall, cruel-eyed slave traders. Here one stopped to make a girl open her mouth to see if her teeth were good and to feel her arm as farmers do sheep in a cattle market. There another made a slave run across the open space—as if he were a pony—just to show his paces.

It was the Zanzibar slave market. As Livingstone watched the traffic in human lives, a slave *dhow,* carrying another three hundred captured Africans, sailed into the port. And he knew that for every one that had come alive to Zanzibar, eight or nine had died rather than be captured or had perished on the voyage.

He ground his teeth with anger at the awful cruelties of the slave traders, and in his heart he grieved for "poor, despised, downtrodden Africa." He was starting on his last long trail—the trail of the slave trade.

He climbed on board the *dhow* that he had hired. For four days the ship sailed southward till it made the mouth of the Rovuma, which runs from the highlands of Central Africa out to the east coast. Finding no landing place, they sailed a little way off to Mikindany Bay, where with much shouting, pushing, and pulling the six camels, three buffaloes, two mules, and four donkeys that were to carry their provisions were landed from the *dhow* by the thirty-six East Indians and Africans who were Livingstone's companions. Chitanè, the dog who was with them, helped by barking.

They set out marching along a narrow path through grass that towered over their heads while the sun beat down fiercely. There was no breeze. They had to cut their way through miles of dense jungle, and they hired some "jolly young Makonde" natives to clear the bamboos and creepers with hatchets. The air was steamy and smothering in the valleys but clearer on the hills.

From a hilltop they saw the Rovuma gleaming like a ribbon of silver along the winding valley. They walked —Indian file—up hill and down again into valleys from village to village along the narrow native furrow paths.

The Indian companions, who were a nuisance and a trouble to Livingstone all the time—though he was always kind to them—beat the donkeys about the head, stuck pointed sticks into the camels, killed the buffalo calf, and were always lazy.

One night, as he sat in the doorway of a hut, he saw two men pass with two women chained, the man behind carrying a gun. The horrors of the slave trade were beginning to come upon him again. They met a woman with a heavy slave-taming stick on her neck—a stick made from the trunk of a young tree. The woman's neck had been placed in the fork of the tree and tied there. She was forced to go about bearing this weight with her. Livingstone bought her from her captor, made her free, and led her back to her people.

Village after village they passed, empty—with all the

131

gardens deserted. The people who had sown the seeds and tilled those gardens, the children who had laughed and played among the village huts were all gone—taken as slaves. Again and again they came on an Arab slave encampment with pens in which the slaves were herded like animals. But if the Arabs heard that Livingstone was coming, they fled, for they knew he lived only to destroy their wicked trade.

Livingstone pushed on and on, often nearly starved in a land once filled with happy, contented villages. Yet he reveled in walking over the hills and along the valleys. His muscles became again "as hard as a board"; his face was bronzed; his quick eyes noted the tracks of animals or the loveliness of the flowers and palms and creepers. Then at night he slept soundly after the long day's walking, though sometimes a chorus of roaring lions would wake him.

At last, after getting higher and higher among the uplands east of Lake Nyasa, one day he saw again the gleam of the blue waters of the bright lake that he had discovered on an earlier journey. The lake was so large that he was reminded of the ocean. He ran down to the beach, threw off his clothes, and rushed into the waves that broke upon the shore.

"It was pleasant," he said, "to bathe in the delicious waters again, hear the roar of the sea, and dash into the rollers."

132

While here—needing more ink to write with—he invented some good blue ink out of the juice of a berry mixed with a chemical.

Livingstone wanted to cross the lake. There were two *dhows* on the lake, both used for carrying slaves, but the slave-trading Arabs refused to let him hire one of them for they feared that he might burn it. Livingstone, therefore, started to walk down the eastern shore around the south end of Lake Nyasa.

As he marched along the sultry path, he saw the skulls and bones of abandoned slaves whitening in the sun. He waded through many brooks and trudged over hills until he came to the south end of the lake, which stretched north like a gigantic caterpillar, three hundred miles long.

Walking there in Mpende's village, Livingstone came to a pen of herded slaves, waiting to be driven to the coast to be sold. Most of them were boys about ten years old. Sick at the thought of these lads having been torn from their fathers and mothers, he longed to go straight off and shake the dust of the village from his feet. Yet he stayed on to give medicine to the sick child of the chief. The boy quickly got better, and Livingstone marched on northward up the west shore of the lake.

Soon after he had started, an Arab slaver in the village of a chief called Marenga drew Musa, one of

Livingstone's men, aside to tell him a crafty story that he hoped would stop Livingstone from going on.

"There is," said the Arab to Musa, "a savage Mazitu chief on the path on which the Doctor is leading you. He is slaying everybody who goes through his land. He will kill you all."

Musa, terrified at this, told the other bearers secretly. Nine of them, with Musa, fled under cover of the night, deserting the one who had led them so far. They went down to the coast and sent home to Britain the story that Livingstone had been killed in a fight. Many people believed this story. A few said that it was not true. An Englishman named Young, who had known Musa years before, disbelieved every word of it and set out to Africa to discover the truth. He swiftly made his way up the Zambezi and the Shire, found that the story was not true, heard how Livingstone had trudged on northward, and returned to Britain to rejoice the people's hearts with the news that Livingstone was alive.

Livingstone did not know about this search or the lies that Musa had told. He only thought of the faithful Makololo of his earlier journeys and wished that they were with him now. He was glad that some of the bearers were still faithful, and he went on with them undaunted.

Their dog, Chitanè, would run from end to end of the line of march, barking at the stragglers, then running forward to his master. Chitanè slept at night at the doorway of Livingstone's tent, ready to spring at any man or animal that should come to hurt his master.

But one day they had to wade waist-deep across a marsh a mile wide. Chitanè bravely started to swim across the marsh though his master thought that he was being carried. The dog struggled on, getting weaker and weaker till at last he sank. Livingstone was very sad at losing his companion.

The slave raiders had left the land like a desert so he could get nothing but African maize to eat. He soaked it in the milk of the goats that he had brought with him. Then the goats were stolen from him in the night. He had to eat the hard maize without milk, and one by one his teeth were loosened and fell out.

"I took my belt up three holes to relieve hunger," wrote Livingstone in his private journal.

He dreamed at night about splendid dinners and good food but woke to find himself hungrier than ever.

Among the faithful bearers was a young African named Baraka, who, because he was careful, was allowed to carry the medicine box. In that box was the quinine that helped Livingstone to fight against the fever. One day another bearer offered to help Baraka by carrying his burden for a stage. This bearer, who had been freed from slavery by Livingstone, returned this goodness by fleeing with the burden into the dense forest, where it was impossible for them to track him down. The medicine box was gone—stolen. Livingstone had now no weapon against fever.

"This loss," said Livingstone, "gnaws at my heart terribly. I feel as if I had now received sentence of death."

Yet he wrote pages in his private journal saying that, after all, the thief of the box could not be called so blamable because he was a rescued slave who had been brought up badly.

A mere skeleton of his sturdy self, sick and lonely, robbed of his goats and his medicine, hungry, stricken with fever, deserted by some of his companions, having lost even his dog, Livingstone tramped on to the village of Chitapangwa, a great chief, who received him with some of his men beating drums furiously and others keeping time with rattles.

After leaving here, he marched on through lovely valleys and high wooded hills, up to a ridge from which he could see, still and peaceful in the morning light, the blue waters of Lake Tanganyika.

He was so ill with fever that he tottered as he walked and was plagued with a singing in the head. He grew worse, floundered outside his tent in his delirium, and fell down insensible, striking his head against a box. His few remaining faithful companions carried him into his hut.

The trail had led Livingstone to the very center of the lake country of Africa. The natives, as he recovered, told him stories of wonderful rivers running through lakes as large as seas. By walking up from Lake Nyasa, he had reached the south end of Lake Tanganyika. He longed to get on to Ujiji, on the east shore of Tanganyika, where there was an Arab settlement. For there he hoped to find letters from his children.

Yet he did not go to Ujiji. He had heard that a mighty river ran out of a mysterious lake to the west of him. Ever since the days when the Pyramids were built in Egypt, long centuries ago, men had wondered where the river Nile rose. Yet no one had ever discovered the place. Livingstone wondered whether he had, at last, come near to that very spot. This made him turn aside and begin his march afresh, although he was tired, fever-stricken, and had not seen a single letter from home for three years.

At last, in November, 1867, he discovered the lake he sought and slept there in the hut of an African fisherman. He sailed on Lake Mweru in fishing canoes and walked its shores till he found that a wide river called the Lualaba flowed out to the north. The river that flows into Lake Mweru on the south is called the Luapula.

The heart of the scout and pathfinder was as lively in Livingstone now that he was fifty-four years old in the highlands of Africa as it had been when he was fourteen on the hills of Scotland. So he could not rest till he knew whence the river Luapula came. The Africans said that it flowed from a great lake that lay farther south.

He said, "I will go and discover that lake."

But, egged on by an Arab trader, all his followers, save five, refused to march. They said, "No, we have had enough marching. When you have found one lake, you say, 'I must find another.' We are tired. We want to go to Ujiji to rest. We will not go on this other journey."

"I will not swerve a hair's breadth from my work while life is spared," Livingstone had declared long before. He stood firm to this now and said that he would go on, whoever lagged behind.

He set his face steadfastly south, with his five companions, who included two faithful boys who would have given their lives for him—Susi and Chumah. On the way they passed a slave caravan. The men, yoked together with chains and slave sticks, were singing.

"Why do they sing when they are in chains?" asked Livingstone.

"They are singing revenge," was the reply. "They sing, 'When we die, the yoke will be off. Our spirits will come back. We will haunt and kill those who have sold us.'"

Then in grim and awful chorus the voices of the

slaves rose and fell in unison as they named the men who had sold them, singing, "We will haunt . . . we will kill. . . ."

At one village on the way, called Kazembe's, Livingstone met an Arab trader, named Mohammed Bogarib, who straightway became his friend. Mohammed fed him with vermicelli and cakes, honey and good coffee, cheering him on his lonely journey. So Livingstone tramped on until he discovered Lake Bangweolo, which is more than a hundred miles wide. Green islands stood up out of the blue water. He set sail upon the lake and landed at these islands, where the natives crowded round this strange thing that they had never seen before —a white man.

Turning from broad Lake Bangweolo, Livingstone tramped back northward to Kazembe's village, where he found Mohammed Bogarib, the Arab who had been so kind to him, just waiting to start for Ujiji, on the shore of Tanganyika. There Livingstone expected to find letters, medicine, fresh clothes, and all the news from England, for he had asked that these things be sent there.

Mohammed set his slave caravan in motion. He was as cruel to the slaves as he was kind to Livingstone, who, stricken with fever and with pneumonia, could not walk and was carried for six weeks on a litter up steep ravines, along forest tracks, across streams, and down the hillsides of Tanganyika to the canoes on the shore of the lake.

The wind was high and gusty, and the waves boomed upon the beach. The canoes could never cross the lake and live. So they hugged the shores of the deep bays of the lake till at last they could cross, and Livingstone was landed in Ujiji.

Cloth and beads had been sent for Livingstone to give to his Africans, and letters, medicine, and papers for himself; but nearly all the stores and every letter except one had been stolen or burned by the Arab slave traders. When he wrote forty letters home and paid carriers to take them to the coast, the servants of the Arabs destroyed every one.

With cruel spite and fiendish cleverness, they tried to cut him off from all touch with Britain. They knew that the story of the horrors of the slave trade, which Livingstone alone of all men living was able to tell the British, would do more to raise the world against their trade and sweep it away than anything else on earth.

Livingstone was surrounded by a ring of snarling foes, who dared not slay him, yet hoped to hold him powerless as in a net.

13 : *Spears in the Bush*

With a proud Arab at their head, a band of Africans, carrying guns and shackles, marched out from Ujiji village. Lying in the shade of the veranda of his little house, David Livingstone, slowly winning back his health, watched them sadly as they passed by on their slave raiding.

His face was furrowed with the pain of a hundred fevers and tanned with the African sun. His mouth was set in grim determination that—when health came back —he would go on with his work, whoever might oppose. Yet his strong face warmed into a smile as his faithful

Chumah came to bring a cup of tea to refresh the beloved Bwana (master).

At nightfall the sound of harsh commands and the crack of whips was heard. It was another Arab returning from a raid with scores of miserable slaves being driven into the village. Livingstone sat on, brooding over the wrongs of Africa—slowly planning to go west into the unknown Manyuema country to find whether the Lualaba was indeed the Congo or the Nile. He heard dim rumors of a great chief who ruled the country on the river and determined to set out to find him. He knew that if he found the hidden sources of the Nile, the whole world would listen to him. And he wanted to tell the world the story of the slave trade.

He roused himself, still weak with fever, and with his followers he took a boat across Lake Tanganyika. All night they rowed, and in the morning they landed on an island, made a fire, cooked breakfast, and took to the boats again. At last, after staying at another islet, they reached the west shore. There they landed and marched through open forest, fording rivers knee-deep.

They came upon hunting parties of Manyuema people, shooting their poisoned arrows—large ones for elephants and buffaloes but small ones, made of strong grass stalks, for smaller animals. He stayed among these people in their villages among the mountains.

The strangest creature of this lovely land of great

mountains, gigantic trees, and deep dells was the soko—
a wild, human-looking ape that beats on its breast as
on a drum, lives on bananas, makes nests in the trees,
kidnaps children and carries them to its nest, crushes
men in its awful grip, and, as Livingstone saw, bites
off their fingers and toes when fighting for its life.

A young soko was given to Livingstone and soon
learned to love him, giving him a cry of welcome when
she saw him, crying if he would not carry her. She was
like a child, covering herself with a mat to sleep and
wiping her face with a leaf for a napkin.

He found the Manyuema all kind to him, except
where the Arabs or their slaves had been. Yet they were
always fighting—one tribe against another.

For the first time in his thousands of miles of tramp-
ing, the Pathfinder's feet failed him. Awful sores came
upon them and prevented him from walking. This kept
him at one place eighty days in a hut. All his companions had left him, save three—Susi, Chumah, and Gard-
ner. Yet he could enjoy sitting under a tree with his
umbrella up in drenching rain, drinking rain water to
quench his thirst, and listening to a tiny green tree frog
that sat by him on a leaf and sang like a bird.

As he went on and reached Bambarre, a village near
the Luama, a tributary of the river Lualaba, he met
slave gangs who had been captured on the other side
of the river.

Captive children would march along with wonderful strength till the sound of dancing and drumming would fall on their ears as they passed some village. It reminded them of home. Then they would sob and waste away with broken hearts.

"I am heartsore," Livingstone confided to his journal, "and sick of human blood."

It was a bright sultry morning on the banks of the Lualaba at Nyangwe market. The river was dotted with canoes laden with Manyuema women bringing to the market their baskets of fruit and fowl, flour and vegetables, salt and pepper. They came by river and forest path till fifteen hundred of them were busily and happily buying and selling, surrounded by their children and friends. Little girls ran about selling cups of water to the thirsty bargainers.

Livingstone walked among them, enjoying the sight and even the noise, with the cocks crowing, the pigs squealing, and the children laughing. He was just strolling away when a shot and a scream broke on his ear. He turned and saw three servants of the slave trader firing right into the thick of the people.

The laughter was changed to shouts of terror as the women threw down their goods and dashed to the canoes. Men and women, wounded with shot, leaped into boats and into the river to swim for the opposite bank, which was nearly three miles off, for the Lualaba was very wide. But, one after another, the heads that dotted the river sank.

Livingstone, in burning anger, clutched his pistol to fire at these murderers. But he held his hand. Had he fired he would have been killed. He did not fear that, but he did a greater thing. Livingstone wrote down the story of that morning. When it reached England, it roused the world more than anything else had ever done to sweep this monstrous slave traffic from under the sun.

Next morning just before starting back eastward to Ujiji, he stood on a height and counted seventeen villages in flames fired by these ruffians.

He and his men on the way back were passing one day along a narrow path with dense bush brushing their elbows on either side. Suddenly there was a rustle among the leaves. A large spear shot through the bush, grazed Livingstone's back, and stuck quivering in the earth. Another spear, hurled from behind a tree by an invisible hand, stabbed the earth scarcely a foot in front of him.

Manyuema savages, thinking that Livingstone was a slave trader who had slain men and burned villages, were out in ambush, set on killing the best friend that they had in the world.

Livingstone marched on and saw in front of him a gigantic tree. It was growing on an anthill that was itself twenty feet high. Fire was burning at its roots, weakening the trunk. He heard a crack, saw the tree shiver and sway in the wind, and then fall toward himself. He turned and rushed back. With a crashing of branches the enormous trunk fell with a thud to the earth a yard behind Livingstone's back, covering him with a cloud of dust.

It was the third hairbreadth escape in that one day.

"Peace! Peace!" cried his scattered attendants as they came back to him. "You will finish all your work in spite of these people and in spite of everything!"

"We had," said Livingstone, "five hours of running the gantlet, waylaid by spearmen, who all felt that if they killed me, they would be revenging the death of relatives. From each hole in the tangled mass we looked for a spear, and each moment we expected to hear the rustle that told of deadly weapons hurled at us.

"I became weary with the constant strain of danger, and—as I suppose happens with soldiers on the field of battle—not courageous, but perfectly indifferent whether I was killed or not."

Livingstone, now very ill, struggled over the mountain range, through dense bush, across running rivers, and then through open forest till he and his men came within sound of the waves breaking on Tanganyika's beach. He had left the Manyuema country.

"I read," he says, "the whole Bible through four times while I was in Manyuema."

He reached Ujiji starved and ill, only "a ruckle of bones," to find that all the stores that he had ordered to be sent there had been sold and the proceeds taken by Shereef, a Moslem tailor of the place.

"I felt in my destitution as if I were the man who went down from Jerusalem to Jericho and fell among thieves. I could not hope for priest, Levite, or Good Samaritan to come by on either side. . . . But when my spirits were at their lowest ebb, the Good Samaritan was close at hand."

There was the sound of guns being fired into the air outside Ujiji. Susi rushed to Livingstone at the top of his speed. Pausing for a moment, he gasped out, "An Englishman! I see him!" and darted off to meet the stranger.

Toward the village there strode a white man at the head of a caravan of African followers. By his side walked a gigantic Negro bearing unfurled the flag of the United States of America. The white man had traveled many thousand miles in search of Livingstone, for news of whom the whole world had now waited for years.

The American was excited beyond words. "What would I not have given," he said afterward, "for a bit of friendly wilderness where I might vent my joy in some mad freak—turning a somersault or slashing at trees! My heart beat fast."

As he walked toward the village, he saw the man for whom he had searched.

"As I advanced toward him I noticed he was pale, that he looked wearied and wan, that he had gray whiskers and mustache, that he wore a bluish cloth cap with a faded gold band on a red ground round it, and that he had on a red, sleeved waistcoat and a pair of gray tweed trousers."

Henry Morton Stanley, the young American, yearned to embrace Livingstone, yet held himself in, and, walking deliberately to him, took off his hat and said, "Dr. Livingstone, I presume?"

"Yes," said Livingstone, with a kind smile, lifting his cap. He had not seen a white face for five years.

They grasped hands—American and Briton in the heart of Central Africa.

Under the eaves of Livingstone's little house Stanley handed him a bag of letters from England—the first that he had received for years. Livingstone chose out one or two by the handwriting on the envelopes, letting documents from statesmen and scholars fall back unopened into the bag. His face beamed as he read them. They were letters from his children.

14 : The Last Trail

Sitting side by side under the eaves of that roof in Ujiji, the men talked.

"You have brought me new life," Livingstone repeated again and again.

He had been eating two tiny meals a day; now he ate four good ones. He laughed "with a laugh of the whole man from head to heel." Sly fun peeped out of the corners of his eyes as he told Stanley quaint and moving stories of his adventures.

Then they rose, as the sun slowly sank behind the mountains across the lake, and walked up and down the shore, breathing the cool breezes that moved on the water and watching the waves beating on the smooth white beach. There Stanley told Livingstone how he had been suddenly telegraphed for by James Gordon Bennett of the New York *Herald* and told to go to Central Africa, to spare no expense but at all costs to find Livingstone if he was alive.

They laughed and chatted again in the market place of Ujiji, telling their adventures as they looked out over the broad silver lake. A cloud of dust showed where a flock of bleating goats and a herd of lowing cattle were being driven in to the market. Up from the boats along the beach came fishermen to sell their catches. Stacks of ivory tusks, baskets of beads, salt, and fruit were sold there by gossiping old African women, the men standing by leaning on their spears while children ran in and out playing and eating bananas.

They set sail on the lake one day in a large canoe, carved from a great mvula tree, with sixteen rowers, and plenty of cloth and beads for money. In the calm green depths of the lake the hippopotami lurked, coming up to breathe and blow close to the canoe, and then ducking again, "as if they were playing hide-and-seek."

At night Livingstone and Stanley landed, set up their tents, and slept, striking tent again at daybreak as the sun called the white mists from the surface of the lake.

In the lovely bays of Tanganyika they saw Africans

fishing from their boats in front of their cozy villages, with the neat gardens and grainfields behind under the shadow of the beautiful hills. On the beach the brown children splashed and paddled fearlessly, with their mothers looking on.

Stones were hurled at them at one place where they wished to land. Stanley wished to fire at the savage people to frighten them. But Livingstone showed that he did not wish this, telling Stanley how often he himself had suffered from such treatment as this, and had found it always due to the cruel treatment of slave traders.

They landed farther along on a spit of sand and made supper. But while they ate it in the fading evening light, they saw parties of savages creeping up from all sides. Hurriedly they took their seats with the rowers in the canoe and pushed off, and not a moment too soon. For in the dusk they saw dark forms creeping over the rocks to the sandy place that they had just left.

On they went northward. Fever struck Stanley down, and Livingstone laid his cool hands on his friend's hot forehead and nursed him back to health.

As Stanley was sleeping during the heat of one day, he was awakened by shouts of, "Master, master, get up, quick! Here is a fight going to begin!"

He sprang up, buckling on his revolver belt. A crowd of angry natives and a drunken youth were threatening

151

to kill the party, thinking that they were Arabs and wishing to avenge a murder committed by Arabs on their tribe.

Dr. Livingstone, who had gone off with his compass, just then came in sight over the brow of a hill with Susi and Chumah. A fight seemed unavoidable. But Livingstone, smiling and baring his arm to show the white skin, said:

"See, I am not an Arab but a white man." In this way he gently quieted the fierce and passionate natives, who let him and Stanley depart in peace.

After going down the lake to Ujiji and spending Christmas there, they started away again in two canoes for Unyanyembe, where Livingstone was to wait while Stanley went to the coast and sent up stores and good bearers for the Pathfinder's last journey.

"Come home with me to England," Stanley had said again and again. "Your family would like to see you, oh, so much!"

"I must finish my task," Livingstone answered, and he wrote in his journal the words that his daughter Agnes had written in her last letter:

"Much as I wish you to come home, I would rather that you finished your work to your own satisfaction than return merely to gratify me."

"Rightly and nobly said, my darling Nannie," wrote her father, his eyes glowing with pride.

At Ujiji all was bustle and excitement as the canoes started, Livingstone ahead, with the British flag flying on a great bamboo at the stern of his boat, while Stanley followed with the Stars and Stripes waving from a still taller flagstaff.

Livingstone, in joke, vowed to cut down the tallest palm he could find so that he could fly the flag of Great Britain higher than that of the States.

"I cannot look at the flags," says Stanley, "without pride that the two Anglo-Saxon nations are represented this day on this great inland sea in the face of wild nature and barbarism."

The boatmen were excited, too. They raced and spurted, shouted and sang, perspired and laughed, groaned and puffed. Stanley had mapped out a way to Unyanyembe that would avoid the dangerous tribes that he had met on the way up. So the boatmen as they rowed sang to celebrate this:

> We have given the Waka the slip! ha! ha!
> The Wavinza will trouble us no more! ho! ho!
> Miorivu can get no more cloth from us! hy! hy!
> And Kiala will see us no more—nevermore! he! he!

They then burst into laughter and pulled with such tremendous power at the oars that the canoes quivered from stem to stern. And while they sped down the lake, their land party on the bank with goats, sheep, and donkeys shared the joy and joined in the song.

153

The land party met them again at a river delta, where they left the lake and struck eastward to Unyanyembe. On the journey they saw herds of graceful giraffes, some seventeen feet high, grazing on the leaves of trees.

At last they reached the village. The time had come for parting.

"'We had a sad breakfast together," said Stanley afterward. "I could not eat, my heart was too full; neither did my companion seem to have an appetite. We found something to do that kept us longer together. At eight o'clock I was not gone, and I had thought to have been off at five in the morning."

At last they grasped hands and said farewell. Stanley, tough traveler as he was, could not keep back his tears.

"For four months and four days," Stanley wrote afterward, "I lived with Livingstone in the same house, or in the same boat, or in the same tent, and I never found a fault in him. . . . Each day's life with him added to my admiration for him. His gentleness never forsakes him; his hopefulness never deserts him. His is the Spartan heroism, the inflexibility of the Roman, the enduring resolution of the Anglo-Saxon. The man has conquered me."

Stanley turned to take his last look at the old hero. Livingstone, with bent head and slow resolute step, turned back to finish his lonely task.

Livingstone was never seen by a white man again.

He waited at Unyanyembe till Stanley's promised stores and bearers should come. Day after day passed, and no news came.

Livingstone watched the whydah (whid'ah) birds feeding their young. "Each little one puts his head on one side as the male bird inserts his bill, chirruping and playing with him. The young ones lift up a feather as a child would a doll, and invite others to do the same, as if saying, 'Come, let us play at making little houses.'"

He also enjoyed seeing the African boys playing with their little bows and arrows. They shot at locusts that settled on the ground. They made play guns of reed, which went off with a trigger and spring, with a cloud of ashes for smoke. Sometimes they made double-barreled guns of clay with cotton fluff for smoke.

In that five months of waiting Livingstone wrote a letter to the New York *Herald,* in which he said of the slave trade those words that stung awake the heart of the world: "All I can say in my loneliness is, may Heaven's rich blessing come down on everyone—American, Englishman, Turk—who will help to heal this open sore of the world."

One day he stood up with eagerness in his face as he saw a line of Africans coming toward him. They were the porters hired by Stanley and sent to Livingstone. His weary waiting was over.

155

With shouting of men and lowing of cattle they started off on the last long trail to find the river Luapula and to discover whether, after all, it was the source of the Nile or the Congo. They went west to Tanganyika, the herds of zebra galloping off as they passed, while now and again the roar of lions filled the bush.

Southward they went and, after Christmas, 1872, plunged through the dark and awful marshes round Lake Bangweolo. The ceaseless rain beat upon their heads. Livingstone suffered agonies of pain through illness and grew weaker day by day. He became, at last, too feeble to wade and often would be lifted from the shoulders of Susi to those of Chumah and other bearers as they crossed the swollen rivers wading chin-deep in the water.

Then his strength left him so that he could not even sit up. His faithful bearers made him a *kitanda*—a kind of hammock slung on a pole borne on men's shoulders.

With tender care—for each jolt of the *kitanda* sent pain through him—those sturdy Africans, Susi and Chumah, with the help of Jacob Wainwright, one of the men sent by Stanley, carried Livingstone, splashing through marsh and walking in the narrow path between the tall grasses.

At last in his journal we find this: "Knocked up quite, and remain—recover—sent to buy milch goats. We are on the banks of the Molilamo."

These are the last words he ever wrote.

They crossed the Molilamo River and slowly, with many rests, paced the way to Chitambo's village in Ilala.

"Stop, put me down," came the feeble voice from the *kitanda* again and again as Chumah bent down to listen to the beloved friend's wish.

They put him down under the broad eaves of a native hut till the new hut that they were building for him was ready.

Villagers came and, leaning upon their bows and spears, gazed at the stricken Pathfinder. They had heard of him in other years, from men who had told them, "He is good. He does not beat his bearers. He has no slaves."

The hut was finished. Susi and Chumah carried him in and laid him down.

"Susi, bring my watch," came the voice.

Susi held the watch in his master's palm while Livingstone slowly turned the key and wound it.

The night fell. A fire burning outside the door cast its glare within the hut.

Just after eleven Susi was called. Livingstone's mind was wandering to the great river that he had set out to reach.

"Is this the Luapula?" he asked.

"No," said Susi, gently, "we are in Chitambo's village near the Molilamo."

157

There was silence. Then the faint voice came:

"How many days is it to the Luapula?"

The Pathfinder was still eager for the river of his quest.

"I think it is three days, Master," replied Susi.

He sighed.

Susi went back to his own hut. A boy, Majwara, stayed with Livingstone to watch. An hour later the boy called Susi, who, holding a candle and the medicine chest near to Livingstone, helped him to select some medicine.

"All right, you can go now," murmured Livingstone.

Just before dawn Majwara called to Susi, "Come to Bwana; I am afraid."

Susi called Chumah and three others.

They entered the hut. By the dim light of the flickering candle, they saw the bowed form of their master kneeling by the bedside, his head buried in his hands on the pillow.

They waited, thinking that he prayed. But the prayer was ended. The Pathfinder had found his Quest. He had crossed the River.

Standing about the dying watchfire, as the cock crew and the dawn broke, the men in whispers planned what they must do. Their love for him made them plan an act of daring and heroic faithfulness.

158

They took his heart and buried it under a mvula tree near Chitambo's village. They embalmed his body, wrapped him in swaths, bound the burden to a pole, and, bearing him shoulder high, carried their leader, now no longer able to guide them, about thirteen hundred miles to the east coast.

Livingstone had made his last march; yet after his death he went on the most wonderful of all his journeys. Let the names of those five immortal brown companions who had been with him since he started from Zanzibar eight years before be written here: Susi and Chumah, Amoda, Abram and Mabruki. With them was the faithful Jacob Wainwright.

They bore him through marsh and river, forest and jungle, over mountain ridges and along the valley paths. They crossed the Luapula where it is four miles wide. They faced hunger and thirst, the spear and gun of enemies, for his sake.

They found as they neared the east coast that the natives all along the path were set on stopping them from carrying the body through their land. So they wrapped it up to look like a traveling bale of cotton and made another package out of fagots of wood to look about like their original burden.

Six men then marched off as if to Unyanyembe with the fagot bundle. The villagers thought that Livingstone was being carried back to the interior, and so allowed

159

the party to go to the coast with its "bale of cotton," which was really their precious charge.

At last they reached the coast. The body was carried to a cruiser and so borne to England while all the world mourned his death.

Livingstone had stood thirty-five years before in the silence of the great nave of the Abbey Church of Westminster, a dark-haired student with bared head before the monuments of the heroes and kings, soldiers and saints, of the Anglo-Saxon race. There, on April 18, 1874, he himself, among the greatest of the "race of hero spirits," was laid to rest.

From that hour until this, no day ever ends without the visitation in that ancient Abbey of men and women or boys and girls who read with reverent eyes the words of brass set in the stone that marks the resting place of David Livingstone.

Epilogue

Under the blazing sun that beats down on Zanzibar stands today a beautiful cathedral, built by free Africans on the site of the old slave market where Livingstone saw shackled men, women, and children being sold like cattle.

In that cathedral African choir boys sing the words that Jesus quoted:

> "He hath sent me to heal the brokenhearted,
> To preach deliverance to the captives, . . .
> To set at liberty them that are bruised."

An African minister reads the lesson: "I am the voice of one crying . . . Make straight the way of the Lord."

The Pathfinder marches on!

A Scottish engineering student, having read Henry Morton Stanley's book *How I Found Livingstone*, picked up a newspaper and read there a letter in which Stanley called for "a practical missionary" to go and help save Africa. Then and there Alexander Mackay wrote to the Church Missionary Society in London these words:

My heart burns for the deliverance of Africa, and if you can send me to any one of those regions that Livingstone and Stanley have found to be groaning under the curse of the slave hunter, I shall be very glad.

Within four months he was on board the S.S. *Peshawar* as she steamed out toward Zanzibar. In the great country of Uganda in Central Africa he laid the foundations of a Christian church, which, in that part of Africa alone, now numbers hundreds of thousands.

Livingstone marches on!

In December, 1938, many African Christian leaders went to Madras in India. There they represented the Christian people of Africa in a great world gathering of Christians of all races and colors who came from some seventy different countries. As these dark, dignified African Christians, including one woman, moved to their places, many of those present must have seen

162

at their head, with the eye of imagination, the sturdy figure of a white man "with his characteristic forward-tread, firm, simple, resolute."

Livingstone marches on!

Many men of the Bechuana people, to whom Livingstone gave so much of his time and affection, fought in Italy and the Near East during World War II. With them were two European and six African chaplains.

The Bechuana churches collected from their people in poor villages and little hamlets twelve hundred dollars to pay for Testaments to send to their soldiers. They sent a cable to the Bible Society in London ordering six thousand Testaments in the Sechuana language. These were packed into a hundred parcels, each containing sixty Testaments, and sent to Italy. The eyes of the Bechuana soldiers sparkled when each was given a Testament that had been paid for by his fellow Christians in Africa.

One of the European chaplains wrote in 1944 about these Bechuana:

The African sees things in terms of the tribe rather than of the individual, and fellowship is a very precious thing to him. The result is that in each company of Bechuana men there is something like a little Christian church, and men are steadily joining it. . . . They are all expected to contribute to their church at home—those African churches of which they are still a part and to which they will return.

163

This same chaplain was about one thousand yards from the line one night in Italy, groping about looking for his men. At last a farm building loomed up black and silent. Hearing a murmur of voices he shouted, "Anybody there?" Getting no answer but just the murmur of voices he called again, "Who's in there?" Still no answer. Then he recognized the murmur. They were saying the Lord's Prayer in Sechuana. (Whoever it was that was outside could wait!) A voice spoke the benediction. Then the chaplain pushed aside the sacking that formed the door and peered inside. Brown faces in the light of a little fire looked up at him with amazement, pleasure, and welcome.

Livingstone marches on!

The most precious possession of the London Missionary Society, which sent David Livingstone to Africa, is a large map of a part of the Zambezi River basin that had never been mapped before. This map is about three feet by four feet in size and was drawn by David Livingstone himself. When war came to Britain in the fall of 1939, this map had been placed in a vault in what was thought to be the safest part of the building, the basement.

In one of the worst attacks of the war in May, 1941, heavy bombs rained down on London. One of them, coming down at an angle, struck the building of the London Missionary Society just above the ground, completely wrecking the room in which the map had been stored for safety. The explosion tore the map into fragments, many of them no larger than a postage stamp.

When the workmen came to clear away the rubble, the secretaries of the Society told them about the loss of Livingstone's map and how much they had prized it. The workmen were interested. "We will find the pieces of that map if we possibly can," they said stoutly. "This war shall not be allowed to stop Livingstone's work, if we can help it."

So as day after day they lifted each shovelful of dust and fragments they sifted it with care and picked out every tiny scrap of blue paper, because Livingstone had drawn his map on paper of that color. When all the pieces of blue paper were fitted together, like a jigsaw puzzle, only one piece about four inches square was missing.

Livingstone marches on!

During that same moonlight night in May, 1941, other bombs hit Westminster Abbey, which is near the London Missionary Society building. Rubble fell on the stone that marks the burial place of David Livingstone, and the sky showed through a gaping hole in the high arched roof above it.

Not long after that night of terror a great service was held in the damaged Abbey. Up through the hole in the roof above Livingstone's grave soared the words of

165

a great hymn, "A Mighty Fortress Is Our God." It was sung by refugees from many European nations, by men and women from the United States and Canada, from India and China and Australia and New Zealand—yes, and by Africans, too. The Africans for whom Livingstone had given his life were taking part in a great service of the universal church with Christians from all parts of the world.

Livingstone marches on!

ABOUT THE AUTHOR

BASIL MATHEWS, born in Oxford, England, lived for many years in London, where he served the British missionary societies as writer, press representative, and editor of news from churches around the world.

For more than a third of a century, beginning with the first world missionary conference in Edinburgh in 1910, Dr. Mathews attended, directed, or reported on a wide range of Christian world meetings. In connection with these conferences, he acquired a knowledge of actual conditions in major European countries, much of the Near East, India, the Far East, and the United States and Canada. He was particularly interested in studying the life of youth in all these countries and for many years was in close touch with students both in the United States and Canada.

The author's first biography for young people, *Livingstone the Pathfinder,* was published in 1912 by the Missionary Education Movement of the United States and Canada. His last book, *Forward through the Ages,* the story of the expansion of Christianity throughout the world, was published in 1950 by the Joint Commission on Missionary Education of the National Council of the Churches of Christ, successor to the Missionary Education Movement, with the imprint of Friendship Press.

ABOUT THE ARTIST

KURT WIESE is famous for his illustrations and has contributed his work to countless publications. He has lived on every continent at some time in his life and has an unusual background of experience that insures authenticity in his drawings of foreign lands. He has illustrated five other Friendship Press books—*Dike against the Sea, Mpengo of the Congo, The Moffats, Many Hands in Many Lands,* and *Face to Face with India.*

ABOUT THE FORMAT

The text of this book is set in Caledonia 11 point leaded four points. Caledonia, a linotype face designed by the distinguished American designer and typographer, W. A. Dwiggins, belongs to the family of printing types called "modern face" by printers. Similar to Scotch Modern in some respects, it is more freely drawn than that letter; and since it was first cut in 1939 it has become one of the most popular and widely used faces in the field of book design.

COMPOSITION: RUTTLE, SHAW & WETHERILL, INC., PHILADELPHIA · OFFSET LITHOGRAPHY AND BINDING: SOWERS PRINTING COMPANY, LEBANON, PENNSYLVANIA · COVERS: AFFILIATED LITHOGRAPHERS, INC., NEW YORK · TEXT PAPER: WARREN'S OLDE STYLE WHITE WOVE.

Typographic design by Margery W. Smith
Binding design by Louise E. Jefferson

A high point in the book is the historic meeting between Livingstone and the intrepid Stanley, who traveled thousands of miles to find the aging missionary. Ailing and feeble, Livingstone expressed the motif of his entire life when he refused Stanley's plea that he return home. For him, there could be no going back. Up to the day he died there was always one more path to explore, one more people to reach and help.

This boo! out a great man and his
rstanding of the
life of David Livingstone
tless young Christians to
e.

ThE JîHOR
eprint of *Livingstone the*
a testimony to the popularity of
and its treatment by the author.
biography for young
wrote. Through-
ally interested in
ments of youth.
aduate of Oxford
taught university
and Canada and
s for young people. His
Forward through the Ages, was
Friendship Press shortly before
1951.

ABOUT THE ARTIST

Kurt Wiese is one of the most highly regarded and prolific illustrators in this country. More than three hundred books feature his distinctive drawings. Recent books he has illustrated for Friendship Press include *The Moffats* and *Face to Face with India.*

FRIENDSHIP PRESS • NEW YORK

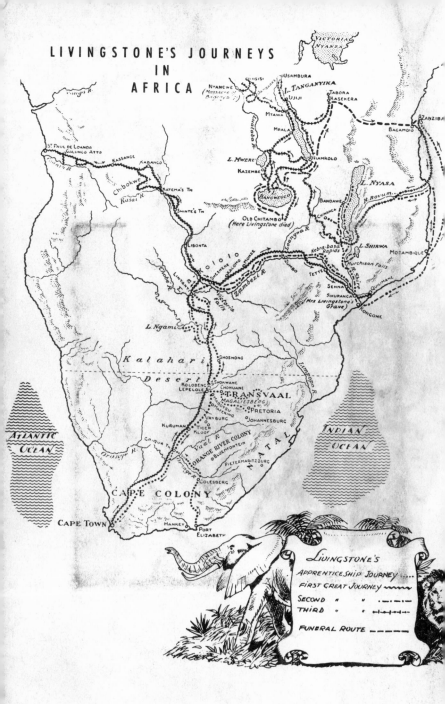

LIVINGSTONE'S JOURNEYS
IN
AFRICA

VICTORIA NYANZA

USAMBURA
L. TANGANYIKA
UJIJI
KASEKERA
TABORA
NYANGWE
(Massacre of Bagenya?)
MTAWA
MPALA
ZANZIBAR
BAGAMOIO

ST. PAUL DE LOANDA
GALUNGO ALTO
KASSANGE
KABANGO
CHIBOKWE
Kusai R.
KATEMA'S Tn.
SHINTE'S Tn.

L. MWERU
KAZEMBE
CHIAMKOLO
L. NYASA
R. ROVUM.

L. BANGWEOLO
BANDAWE
OLD CHITAMBO
(Here Livingstone died)

LIBONTA
LOLOLO
CHISENGA
GALONGO MONTE
KEBRA-BASA RAPIDS
L. SHIRWA
MURCHISON FALLS
MOZAMBIQUE

Zambezi R.
Victoria Falls
TETTE
SENNA
SHUPANGA
(Mrs. Livingstone's Grave)
KONGONE
QUILIMANE

L. Ngami
SHOSHONG

Kalahari Desert
SHORWANE
KOLOBENG
LEPELOLE
CHONUANE
TRANSVAAL
MAGALIESBERG
PRETORIA
MABOTSA
LOTLAKANE
JOHANNESBURG
Limpopo R.

KURUMAN
VRYBURG
TIGEO KLOOF
ORANGE RIVER COLONY
BLOEMFONTEIN
NATAL
PIETERMARITZBURG

Atlantic Ocean
Orange R.
GRIQUA Tn.
Vaal R.
COLESBERG
CAPE COLONY

Indian Ocean

CAPE TOWN
HANKEY
PORT ELIZABETH

LIVINGSTONE'S
APPRENTICESHIP JOURNEY ....
FIRST GREAT JOURNEY ~~~~~~
SECOND " " ·—·—·—
THIRD " " +—+—+—
FUNERAL ROUTE — — —

Paper $1.95